NEW SCOTLAND,
NEW POLITICS?

D1283662

The Authors

Lindsay Paterson is Professor of Educational Policy at the University of Edinburgh. His books include *The Scottish Electorate* (Macmillan), *A Diverse Assembly* (Edinburgh University Press), *The Autonomy of Modern Scotland* (Edinburgh University Press) and *Politics and Society in Scotland* (Macmillan).

Alice Brown is Professor of Politics at the University of Edinburgh and Co-Director of the Governance of Scotland Forum. Her publications include *The Scottish Electorate* (Macmillan) and *Politics and Society in Scotland* (Macmillan).

John Curtice is Professor of Politics at the University of Strathclyde and Deputy Director of the ESRC Centre for Research into Elections and Social Trends. His publications include *On Message* (Sage).

Kerstin Hinds is a Senior Researcher at the National Centre for Social Research in Edinburgh.

David McCrone is Professor of Sociology and Convenor of the Unit for the Study of Government in Scotland. His recent books include *The Sociology of Nationalism* (Routledge), *Scotland the Brand* (Polygon), *Understanding Scotland* (Routledge), and *Politics and Society in Scotland* (Macmillan).

Alison Park is Director of the National Centre for Social Research, Scotland. Her publications include the British Social Attitudes report series.

Kerry Sproston is a Researcher at the National Centre for Social Research.

Paula Surridge is a Lecturer in Sociology at the University of Salford. She is co-author of *The Scottish Electorate* (Macmillan).

NEW SCOTLAND,
NEW POLITICS?

Lindsay Paterson, Alice Brown,
John Curtice, Kerstin Hinds,
David McCrone, Alison Park,
Kerry Sproston and Paula Surridge

POLYGON
AT EDINBURGH

© Lindsay Paterson, Alice Brown, John Curtice, Kerstin Hinds,
David McCrone, Alison Park, Kerry Sproston and Paula Surridge, 2001

Polygon at Edinburgh
An Imprint of Edinburgh University Press Ltd
22 George Square, Edinburgh

Typeset in Bembo
by Pioneer Associates Ltd, Perthshire, and
printed and bound in Great Britain by
Creative Print and Design, Ebbw Vale, Wales

A CIP Record for this book is available
from the British Library

ISBN 1 902930 25 8 (paperback)

The right of Lindsay Paterson, Alice Brown, John Curtice,
Kerstin Hinds, David McCrone, Alison Park, Kerry Sproston and
Paula Surridge to be identified as authors of this work has been
asserted in accordance with the Copyright, Designs and
Patents Act 1988.

CONTENTS

LIST OF TABLES

—·wwwPⓅAwww·—

Tables refer to Scotland and to 1999 unless otherwise stated.

LIST OF TABLES

ACKNOWLEDGEMENTS

The main survey used in this book – the Scottish Parliamentary Election Survey 1999 – was financed by the UK Economic and Social Research Council (grant number R000238065). The ESRC has also been involved in funding most of the other surveys on which the book draws: see the Appendix. The authors are grateful for their support. They would like to thank Ann Mair of the Social Statistics Laboratory of Strathclyde University for help in gaining access to the data, and the staff of the National Centre for Social Research – especially Katarina Thomson – for their advice during the project. They are also grateful for the comments of John Hills of the London School of Economics on draft versions of Chapters 8 and 9, and for the comments of people who attended a seminar in Edinburgh in February 2000 on the topics of the book.

1

INTRODUCTION

The setting up of the Scottish Parliament had three aims, depending
on the political stance of its advocates. The aim officially endorsed by
leading members of the UK Labour government was to keep
Scotland in the Union. Diametrically opposed to that was the aim of
the Scottish National Party and other supporters of Scottish independence: a devolved Parliament would be the first step towards
breaking the Union. In between was majority opinion in Scotland,
especially in the Labour Party and the Liberal Democrats: the aim of
providing Scottish solutions to Scottish domestic problems and
fostering distinctiveness within the Union.

This book analyses these and related matters. How far have the first
elections to the Parliament expressed a distinctive Scottish political
opinion? What role did the new proportional electoral system play
in facilitating this? How far is there a distinctive Scottish opinion on
policy issues? What impact has the existence of a Scottish Parliament
had on national identity and on attitudes to the Union?

These questions are studied using unique surveys of people in
Scotland. The year 1999 has no precedent in Scottish politics, and
understanding the significance of the political landscape that is now
unfolding requires new evidence, new analysis and new methods of
understanding. The book discusses the significance of the first elections to the new Scottish Parliament, and draws on a new source of

data, the first in a series of social surveys of voters in Scotland, relating it to previous surveys of Scottish voters in UK elections; thus the book offers an interpretation of what happened in 1999 and some indications of where these events may be taking Scotland.

The elections on 6 May 1999 were unprecedented in several ways: not only were they the first democratic elections to any kind of Scottish Parliament, they were the first national elections in Britain to be conducted wholly by any version of proportional representation (along with the first elections on the same day to the National Assembly for Wales). They were also the first elections in Britain to a legislature that enjoyed the endorsement of a clear referendum decision, with all the high public expectations which that raised.

The outcome, too, had few parallels in UK politics, and had implications that were being felt within a year of the Parliament's assumption of power. Because of the proportional system, no party won an absolute majority, and so the new government was a coalition between the Labour Party and the Liberal Democrats (see Table 2.1 in Chapter 2). That immediately had an effect on Scottish public policy. The first instance was the issue of student finance in higher education: since all the non-Labour parties in the Parliament were committed to ending student fees, Labour was forced to concede an independent inquiry into the matter, which in due course has led to the abolition of fees and to the partial reintroduction of student grants.

Party proportionality also led to three other changes. The Scottish National Party was finally represented in numbers that matched its share of the vote (something it has never managed to achieve under the first-past-the-post electoral system), and so became the official opposition. This has given a new public exposure to SNP politicians, and has ensured that the question of Scotland's future constitutional status remains high on the political agenda. The Parliament was never likely to have settled down into being a tame regional legislature, but the presence of so many SNP members ensured that this was impossible.

The Conservatives, too, benefited from the voting system, and may thus have started a slow recovery from the complete wipeout of their representation in the 1997 UK general election. They are the only public voice of the substantial minority of Scottish opinion that subscribes to broadly right-wing ideas.

Finally, proportionality gave representation to two smaller, vociferous parties – the Scottish Socialists and the Greens – with a very striking effect on debate. The Greens' Robin Harper has raised environmental matters in more searching ways than has ever happened before in a UK legislature. The Scottish Socialists had a famous legislative triumph when Tommy Sheridan's bill to reform debt-recovery methods was endorsed in the face of government scepticism. That very visible success for a small radical party is an achievement unmatched even by the British Communist Party at the high point of its parliamentary influence from the 1920s to the 1940s.

The outcome of the elections did not affect only parties, however. Thirty-seven per cent of the members of the Parliament are female, more than twice as large a proportion as at Westminster, giving Scotland proportionately more female legislators in its national Parliament than any country in the world outside Scandinavia. This result was due mainly to the Labour Party (with half its MSPs being women) and the SNP (43 per cent). One result has been an attention in the Parliament, never achieved in Westminster, to issues of domestic violence. Another has been a firmer insistence on civil liberties than would probably otherwise have been the case: for example, during the long arguments about whether the Parliament should repeal legislation – 'Section 2a' – that forbade local authorities (and hence local authority schools) from promoting homosexuality, women in the Parliament and in the government recurrently appeared to be taking a more liberal line than the majority of their male counterparts.

On the other hand, despite the fairly high proportion of women, and the broader spread of ages than in Westminster, the Parliament remains embarrassed by its lack of any member of a visible ethnic minority, and – as in all legislatures – by the very strongly middle-class social origins of its members (Cavanagh *et al.* 2000). The success of the campaign to get more women into the Parliament is likely to inspire similar campaigns for other excluded groups.

How are people reacting to the political events preceding and surrounding the Scottish Parliamentary elections? What did the experience of a new electoral system mean? What do the electorate expect the Parliament to do? How does this institutional outcome of thirty years of nationalist or quasi-nationalist campaigning relate to people's sense of national identity? What are people's views about the future of the Union? And why did quite a large proportion – 40 per cent – of the electorate not vote at all? The new context needs new means of investigation. This book reports on the results of the Scottish Parliamentary Election Survey, an intensive examination of the views of a representative sample of almost 1500 people living in Scotland, conducted in the couple of months following the 1999 elections. The survey is intended to be the first in a series of annual surveys of Scottish social attitudes, running parallel to the widely respected British Social Attitudes Surveys that have been carried out annually since 1983 (Jowell *et al.* 1999a). The Scottish Parliamentary Election Survey and its successors not only allow us to analyse Scottish views on a more reliable basis than hitherto (1500 interviews being a much firmer basis for discussion than the roughly 300 Scottish interviews which the BSAS can afford, a typical problem of UK or British surveys for analysis of Scotland). They also allow distinctively Scottish questions to be asked, a particularly important feature as the Scottish voting system, system of government and increasingly also social policy come to diverge from those in England or in Britain as a whole. Nevertheless, by retaining a large core of questions that are common to the Scottish and British surveys, systematic comparisons can continue to be made. Moreover, the new survey series opens up the opportunity, if funding allows, of linking Scotland into the regular International Social Survey Programme, an international collaboration among surveys of public attitudes in thirty-one countries (Jowell *et al.* 1998). If that can be achieved, Scottish views will be able to be set in a fully international context for the first time ever.

We can also relate the results of the new survey to the surveys that were carried out in Scotland at the time of the UK general elections of 1997, 1992, 1979 and 1974, and to surveys of people in Scotland (and Wales) that were carried out after the referendums of 1997. These earlier surveys, although not planned as part of a series, do allow some investigation of how Scottish attitudes have been changing over quite a long period of time. Like these surveys and the British Social Attitudes Survey, the Scottish Parliamentary Election Survey was carried out by the National Centre for Social Research. Further technical information about all the surveys is given in an Appendix.

The surveys are not an attempt to copy what regular opinion polls do – to take, at frequent intervals, the public view on issues of the day. Rather, the surveys' emphasis is on tracking the presence (or absence) of any underlying changes in people's attitudes and values over time. In other words, while the polls chart changes in the immediate political weather, our task is to monitor and explain changes in the more general social and political climate.

Carrying out research on the new Scotland matters if Scotland wants to have a better-informed public debate about policy – one of the underpinning principles of the aspiration to a new politics. Donald Dewar, Scotland's first First Minister, typified this view when he said a couple of months after the referendum in 1997 that 'I am genuinely anxious to . . . make sure that people get a Parliament with open doors and open procedures in which their views . . . will have their due weight' (Dewar 1998: 8). Allowing public views to influence public policy in Scotland has been one of the longstanding reasons which advocates of a Parliament have cited in its favour (Paterson 1998: 2–4). Scottish public opinion matters more now than ever before. The Parliamentary committees have been seeking evidence on legislation and on other matters of public concern. Most government ministers have entered into this spirit by allowing much longer periods of consultation than hitherto on draft legislation, consultation that also has the aim of reaching social groups that have not usually been influential in the past. And on some very controversial matters, public opinion has tangibly influenced outcomes. One example is the public scepticism of the government's proposal to repeal Section 2a (Section 28 in England and Wales), which is the main reason why repeal was accompanied by a revision of the guidelines for teaching about sex and sexuality in schools. The resulting compromise seems to have satisfied most people, even though a majority were apparently opposed to repeal: the new guidelines have probably reassured parents, while also recognising that – according to polls – a large majority of Scots are tolerant of diverse sexual lifestyles. Another example – drawing on data that are further analysed in Chapter 8 here – was provided by the conclusions of the independent committee of inquiry into student finance, which were influenced by the evidence from this survey that people in general cared more about the withdrawal of student grants than about fees.

Informing the policy process is an important part of what the new series of Scottish Social Attitudes Surveys intends to do, and is an important part of this book. But it is not the only role for this work. Equally significant is the scope for analysing whether and to what extent Scottish politics is becoming distinctive. Is the Parliament really being more democratically responsive than Westminster? Do people really behave differently in a Scottish, compared with a UK, election? Do they behave differently when given the chance to use a proportional electoral system? Which segments of the electorate are most inclined to change their practice? How do voters balance the demands they make on the Scottish, UK and indeed European legislatures? Fully answering political questions such as these will, of course, take many years, but this book makes a start.

There is also the very interesting and politically potent matter of how Scottish social attitudes compare with those in the rest of the UK. During the long period of Conservative rule between 1979 and 1997, it was frequently claimed that Scotland had quite different views from England – more left-wing, or more communitarian, or more liberal. Then some scepticism was expressed, largely on the grounds that, in fact, English voters never stopped being broadly social democratic even while voting in large proportions for the government of Margaret Thatcher (Brown *et al.* 1998: 95–100; Curtice 1996). In a sense, the setting up of a Scottish Parliament is premised on some distinctiveness of Scottish views, and certainly the very existence of a separate legislative process and semi-independent government makes further divergence likely.

Of equal interest to comparing Scotland with its large and powerful neighbour is comparing it with other small nations and regions around Europe and beyond. This book should, we hope, be of interest to people studying politics and social attitudes in places such as Wales, Northern Ireland, the autonomous communities of Spain, the French regions, the German Länder, the Belgian communities and the Canadian provinces. Does having an assembly with strong legislative autonomy – as in Scotland, Northern Ireland, Catalonia, the Länder, Belgium, and Quebec – respond to or influence public attitudes in different ways to the weaker administrative assemblies in Wales, the French regions and some of the Spanish communities? Will national identity in Scotland now develop in the same way as in Catalonia after it received substantial autonomy in 1980 – a growth in dual identity (Scottish and British, like Catalan and Spanish) – or will Scotland continue to show much stronger levels of national (Scottish) attachment than Catalonia? Will the electoral strength of the SNP nudge it towards the cautious constitutional reformism of most Catalan nationalists, or towards the radical separatism of the Parti Québecois? Will Scotland offer a model of non-violent politics to its near-neighbour Northern Ireland, and to other areas such as the Basque country where the campaign for autonomy has been much more divisive than in Scotland? On the other hand, can Scotland learn from the experiences in all these other places about how a small nation can enjoy the benefits of autonomy without risking isolation? This book only begins to address these complex questions, but it seeks to advance the process that, over time, might help Scotland to take its place in an international debate about national identity, autonomy and interdependence.

This book has ten chapters. The second provides a summary narrative of the campaigns for the elections in 1999. Chapters 3, 4 and 5 examine in depth how voters responded to the opportunity to elect a new institution – how important they regarded the elections as being, who voted for which party or combination of parties, and what impact the new electoral system had on voters' choices. Chapter 6 asks whether the Parliament has helped keep the UK united, or whether it has encouraged voters to seek greater Scottish autonomy. Chapter 7 looks at national identity, and asks whether it is relevant to political attitudes in Scotland and how it might be changing. Chapter 8 investigates what kinds of social policy Scotland seems to want from its new Parliament, and Chapter 9 examines the particularly high-profile and controversial issue of Scottish education. The final chapter then draws the strands together, assessing the significance for the political parties in Scotland, and asking also what the implications of the analysis are for the future development of Scotland's and the UK's constitution.

2

THE SCOTTISH PARLIAMENTARY
ELECTION OF 1999

INTRODUCTION

The first election for the Scottish Parliament held in May 1999 has provided something akin to a laboratory for political and social scientists. It is extremely rare that the opportunity exists to study the setting up of a new parliament with a new electoral system, especially when such major constitutional reforms have taken place in peaceful circumstances. But such an event is much more than an academic exercise. It represents a crucial moment in Scottish political history that will have an impact on politics and society in Scotland. The constitutional changes that it has heralded also have far-reaching implications for politics in other parts of the UK.

The establishment of the new parliament follows a long campaign in Scotland stretching over many years – some would say since the Treaty of Union in 1707 when its predecessor was dissolved. In more recent history, constitutional change has occurred very rapidly in the period following the Labour Party's return to office at the general election in May 1997. The new government moved swiftly in publishing a White Paper on devolution in July 1997 (Scottish Office 1997) before holding a two-question referendum in September 1997. When the majority of people voting in Scotland responded positively to both the referendum questions, the Scotland Bill was published at the end of 1997, followed by the Scotland Act one year later (Stationery Office 1998). With the remit to draft standing orders and procedures for the new parliament, a cross-party Consultative Steering Group (CSG 1998) was formed and reported to the then Secretary of State, Donald Dewar, in December 1998. Soon after the first election on 6 May 1999, the new politicians – Members of the Scottish Parliament (MSPs) – took their seats on 12 May, a coalition government was formed on 14 May and the Parliament was officially opened by the Queen on 1 July. The opening of the Parliament was described by Sir David Steel, the Presiding Officer, as 'the most significant political achievement in Scotland for nearly 300 years' (Steel 1999). For Donald Dewar, the First Minister, it was 'a new stage on a journey begun long ago and which has no end' (*The Scotsman* 2 July 1999).

This chapter sets the scene and the context for the detailed analysis of the first Scottish parliamentary election that follows. It provides a discussion of the process of constitutional reform in Scotland leading up to the 1999 election campaign and an overview of the election results.[1] It also begins to answer the questions with which we are concerned throughout the book, by examining whether the election campaign and its outcome inaugurated a new Scottish politics. Was there evidence of a new party system emerging, not only in the sense of different voting patterns but also in the formal and informal alliances which parties made with each other over particular policy issues? Did the parties start to think about their Scottish identity in new ways? Did the electoral outcome make a distinctive policy agenda more likely in Scotland? Did the outcome of the election signal a new role for women in Scottish politics? What new roles for civil society are opened up by the new legislature? And does the new constitutional settlement mark the end of the constitutional question in Scottish politics, or simply the beginning of a new phase? We start to look at these questions here, and they run right through the subsequent chapters as well.

ORIGINS OF THE NEW SETTLEMENT

The origins of the scheme proposed for the Scottish Parliament, including the electoral system, have their roots in the long campaign for a parliament, and are illustrated, in part, through the work of the Scottish Constitutional Convention (SCC). The Convention, a product of the Campaign for a Scottish Assembly/Parliament, and its report entitled *A Claim of Right for Scotland*, convened meetings over the period 1989 to 1995 (Harvie and Jones 2000). It provided a forum for political parties, campaigning groups and civic organisations to develop their proposals for a devolved parliament. As Denver *et al.* (2000) remind us, the idea of Conventions has a long history in the home-rule movement, but such bodies in the 1920s and 1940s had failed to make significant progress. The work of the contemporary Convention is perhaps best divided into two periods, one predating the 1992 general election and the other following it. The two key political parties involved – the Scottish Labour Party and the Scottish Liberal Democrats – were able to reach broad agreement on the type of parliament they wished to see established, in terms of its ethos and legislative powers. They broadly agreed that the Parliament should have legislative power over all the areas that were administered by the Scottish Office, and they eventually agreed also that it should be financed mainly by a block grant from the UK government, as the Scottish Office was. The only departure from that would be a very limited power to vary the basic rate of income tax.

Compared with these areas of relatively straightforward agreement, the parties had different approaches to electoral reform. There was great resistance in some quarters of the Scottish Labour Party to any shift towards a more proportional electoral system. For their part, the Scottish Liberal Democrats advocated the benefits of the Single Transferable Vote. The agreement reached before 1992 and published in the document *Towards Scotland's Parliament* was deliberately vague in this and other respects. On the return of the Conservative Party to government, the Convention struggled to keep the home-rule parties together, and it set up a Commission in 1993 with a view to resolving some of the more contentious issues. Many of the Commission's recommendations were later to be found in the Convention's final report, *Scotland's Parliament, Scotland's Right*, pub-lished in 1995. In the intervening period negotiations had continued between George Robertson and Jim Wallace as the leaders of their respective parties in which a deal was struck on the size of the parliament and the electoral system to be adopted. The Convention then recommended a Scottish Parliament of 129 members, to be elected under the Additional Member System of proportional repre-sentation (discussed further below and in Chapter 5) (Scottish Constitutional Convention 1995).

There was also disagreement over how to get a higher proportion of women in the Parliament than there was at Westminster. Following sustained pressure from the women activists campaigning under the umbrella of the Women's Co-ordination Group, an Electoral Agree-ment was reached between the parties in which they committed themselves to the principle of equal representation in the first parliament and to field an equal number of men and women as candidates in winnable seats (Brown 1998).

Although academic commentators have formed different conclu-sions on the impact of the Convention and the extent to which its final report was a blueprint for the Scotland Act that followed, there is no doubt that the process of negotiation which took place over the years helped build broad political acceptance of the scheme. As Denver *et al.* argue, it also provided a framework and 'deepened Labour's commitment to devolution' (Denver *et al.* 2000: 36). The work conducted in the Convention meant that a considerable amount of planning, discussion and agreement had already taken place between many of the key political players long before the 1997 general election and the new Labour government's plans for constitutional change had been announced. As Himsworth and Munro (1998: x) put it, the Convention's 'work over a period of years in progressively developing a scheme for constitutional reform meant that a sympathetic government could import the proposals more or less wholesale. . . . The experience of co-operation between Labour and the Liberal Democrats . . . was taken as a model and encourage-ment to further collaboration in plotting constitutional reforms, both before and after the general election of May 1997.'

It was recognised at this early stage that, in agreeing to a more proportional electoral system, the Scottish Labour Party, accustomed to being the dominant party in Scotland in terms of local council and Westminster and European parliamentary seats, was conceding the likelihood of an overall majority in the new institution. A less charitable interpretation, of course, is that Labour was also ensuring, as best it could, that no other party, specifically the Scottish National Party, was likely to achieve an overall majority in future elections. Nevertheless, the concession being made by Labour, and the efforts required to persuade some key players in the Labour movement of the need to shift their position on electoral reform, should not be underestimated. In their account of 'the road to home rule', Chris Harvie and Peter Jones argue that reaching agreement was 'slow and tortuous' and that depriving Labour of the prospect of running a devolved Scotland on its own 'needed the most careful wooing of trade union delegations' (Harvie and Jones 2000: 154–5).

The Scottish National Party were conspicuous by their absence from the Convention. Although the SNP had been proponents of Conventions in the past, the decision was taken to withdraw after the first meeting of the SCC. It was argued that the new body was likely to be dominated by the Labour Party, even although some concessions had been made in terms of SNP representation, and that participation might compromise the nationalists' policy of 'Independence in Europe'. When the Convention launched its report on St Andrew's Day in 1995, the SNP and the Conservatives published their own positions on the constitution. Opposing the devolution scheme agreed by the other two parties, they offered options at different sides of the constitutional scale; on the one hand the SNP articulated their plans for 'Independence in Europe' and a 200-member parliament, and, on the other, the Conservatives reasserted the case for maintaining the status quo.

Not surprisingly, the constitutional question was a key feature of the 1997 general election in Scotland and dominated the media coverage (Brown 1997). The first-past-the-post electoral system worked in favour of the Scottish Labour Party but to the detriment of the Conservative Party who, in spite of gaining over 17 per cent of the vote, lost all their seats in Scotland. The big question following the election was 'would Labour deliver its pre-election promises on the constitution?'. Sceptics were surprised when Labour published the White Paper on Devolution in July soon after the election in May. It contained few surprises, except perhaps that it was written in an uncharacteristically accessible style for a government document and turned out to be a bestseller for the publishers. Although there was disappointment that some functions, such as broadcasting and equal opportunities legislation, had not been devolved, the White Paper received wide endorsement. The proposals bore a strong resemblance to the Convention's scheme, the main difference being that the areas over which the parliament would have legislative competence were not articulated. Instead, the approach taken was one that had been recommended in a report produced by the Constitution Unit. Writing in *Scottish Affairs* in 1996, Graham Leicester of the Constitution Unit drew attention to the likely practical and constitutional difficulties should the government decide to list all the powers to be devolved (Leicester 1996). It was decided to adopt the approach recommended by the Unit, namely to set out the powers reserved to Westminster, such as foreign and defence policy, fiscal, economic and monetary policy, employment legislation and social security. All other areas were to be the responsibility of the Scottish Parliament, which meant that the new body would have legislative responsibility for a broad range of policies including education (from pre-school to higher), health, local government and local economic development, social work, housing, law and home affairs, agriculture and fisheries, environment and transport.

REFERENDUM CAMPAIGN

The Labour Party had stated that it was their intention to hold a referendum on the constitutional question should they win the general election. It would have two questions: one on the principle of a parliament, and one on the tax powers. This decision was made in the summer of 1996 and caused considerable controversy in Scotland at the time, being interpreted by critics as yet another example of Labour's weak attachment to devolution. Labour's gamble paid off in terms of its impact both before and after the result. Before 11 September, the date set for the referendum, the campaign for a double 'Yes' (to the two questions) provided a vehicle for a broad coalition among home rulers, a campaign which crucially included the SNP. It also helped marginalise the Conservatives as the only party against change. It was a rare moment indeed for Labour and the SNP to be on the same side, publicly, in a constitutional campaign under the umbrella organisation Scotland Forward. The campaign also included representatives from campaigning groups and civic organisations that had supported the work of the Convention. In contrast, the opposition forces, organised under the Think Twice campaign, had great difficulty in harnessing an equivalent level of support and financial resources.

The unexpected death of Princess Diana at the end of August

caused campaigners for a double Yes vote to fear that this would have a detrimental effect on the outcome. In the event, over 60 per cent of voters in Scotland took part in the referendum: of these, 74 per cent agreed that there should be a Scottish Parliament, and 63 per cent answered in favour of a parliament with tax-varying powers (Denver *et al.* 2000). In the light of such public endorsement of the two questions posed, most opposition to reform was crushed. The result also helped ease the passage of the Scotland Bill, published in November 1997, through the Houses of Parliament. It was, of course, aided by the size of Labour's majority in the House of Commons (Himsworth and Munro 1998: xi).

When the Scotland Act was published one year later its first clause began with the memorable words 'There shall be a Scottish Parliament.' (Stationery Office 1998). The stage was now set for the first election.

PREPARING FOR THE FIRST ELECTIONS

Although agreement had been reached on the electoral system to be adopted for the first elections to the Scottish Parliament, it took some time for the details and the true implications of a more pro-portional system to penetrate. To help raise awareness among voters in Scotland, and to try and achieve a high turnout, the Scottish Office launched an information campaign targeted at the press and broadcast media, and published leaflets. Factsheets were distributed to households explaining the voting system. They described the Additional Member System as 'a type of proportional representation' where 'the share of seats each party receives in the Parliament will reflect as closely as possible its level of support among voters' (Scottish Office 1 1999). Voters were to have two votes: one to elect a constituency MSP using the Westminster parliamentary constituencies (plus an additional seat to allow for separate constituencies for Orkney and Shetland); and the other to vote for a political party (or a candidate standing as an individual) using Scotland's then eight European constituencies – usually referred to as the regional vote. The seventy-three constituency MSPs were to be elected by the first-past-the-post system, with the other fifty-six MSPs elected from closed party lists – seven from each of the European regions – in order to correct for disproportionality in the constituency section. (The electoral system is discussed further in Chapters 3 and 5.)

For activists within the political parties, the electoral implications of a more proportional voting process began to register. Uncertainty rose as attempts were made to calculate the likely response of the electorate to a system that allowed them two votes. Voters had an additional choice to make on 6 May 1999 – to cast a vote in the local council elections, still operating under the first-past-the-post system, a factor that added to the confusion and speculation about the parliamentary results. Translating the results of the 1997 general election, and assuming that votes were cast for the same party on the constituency and regional ballots – an assumption that was highly implausible – it was calculated that, as predicted, no party would gain an overall majority. Although Labour would still be the main beneficiary in such a scenario, they would be two seats short of an overall majority. A much more credible scenario, and one supported by opinion poll data, was that voters would exercise choice, and split their allegiance between the constituency and the additional or list seat. A study carried out by Dunleavy *et al.* (1997) provided further evidence that voters would use the new system, and that ticket-splitting would have a significant impact on the distribution of seats between the parties.

During the run-up to the elections, other changes were under way within the political parties both in terms of their internal organisation and also in relation to their selection processes for nominating prospective candidates. The four main political parties adopted what they claimed were more professional recruitment techniques to attract strong candidates. The Labour Party's selection process was singled out for particular criticism by the media on the grounds of alleged political bias, although a more balanced investigation would have revealed high-profile casualties in all the parties. The rejection of Dennis Canavan, the sitting Labour MP for Falkirk West, and his decision to stand as an independent candidate, helped fuel media speculation and the controversy surrounding Labour's selection process.

In order to help ensure that women were not excluded from the new parliament, the women's movement in Scotland continued to campaign to put the issue on the political agenda. The parties responded by stating their aim to attract more women to come forward for selection, although this rhetoric was not always matched with measures to ensure more women candidates. Labour was the only party to adopt a specific mechanism to achieve gender balance by 'twinning' parliamentary constituencies to allow both men and women to stand for election. Under this scheme, the woman with the highest number of votes and the man with the highest number of votes would be selected as the two candidates to represent the twinned seats.

The Scottish Liberal Democrats, Labour's partners in the Convention and signatories of the Electoral Agreement on gender balance, initially proposed a scheme that two men and two women should stand for selection in each constituency, and that the additional or 'top up' seats should be 'zipped' to redress any imbalance in gender composition (that is, the list should alternate women and men). However, the party failed to achieve an equal number of men and women for constituency seats and later decided not to implement the proposed 'zipping' mechanism at their conference in March 1998, despite the support given to this strategy by the leader, Jim Wallace (and despite doing so in the election to the European Parliament a month after the Scottish election). The stated reason was that the party had taken legal advice to the effect that the policy of 'zipping' could be subject to an appeal to the Industrial Tribunal under the terms of the Sex Discrimination Act. Pressure on the Labour Party to find ways of exempting the selection processes of political parties from this legislation by inclusion of an appropriate clause in the Scotland Act was unsuccessful in spite of support from Labour MPs such as Maria Fyfe and Malcolm Chisholm.

The Scottish National Party also moved away from its intention to 'zip' party lists as a way of achieving greater gender balance when the proposal was defeated at its party conference in May 1998. Nevertheless, women's representation became an issue over which there was some competition between Labour and the SNP. The Minister for Women at the time, Helen Liddell, used every opportunity to compare the SNP unfavourably with Labour in this regard. Although not official policy, the SNP did place women at the upper end of their party lists, a practice which was to result in a significant proportion of women MSPs in the Parliament (see Table 2.2 below). The Conservative Party maintained their opposition to special measures for selecting women candidates on the basis that to do so would be patronising to women and against the principles of selecting on merit.

THE ELECTION CAMPAIGN

As the campaign by the political parties to win support in the election gathered force, the collaboration between the pro-home rule parties soon dissolved. With some opinion polls in 1998 putting the SNP ahead of Labour (McCrone 1999), there was significant nervousness in Labour's ranks, and old rivalries between the two parties surfaced. Prominent players in the Labour Party, including Donald Dewar, used the occasion of the Scottish conference in March 1999 to attack the SNP and to warn of the dangers of a costly 'divorce' from the rest of Britain. In such a climate the 'new politics' associated with the Scotland Forward referendum campaign were no longer in evidence.

Most commentators were to declare the campaign a rather dull affair, initially finding few areas of policy to separate the parties, apart from the different constitutional options on offer. The parties too seemed tired in facing the electorate so recently after a general election and the referendum campaign. There was little evidence that the electoral system had significantly altered the rules of the party political game. In spite of the scope for tactical voting, the key message to the electorate from all the major parties was that they should vote twice for them on both the constituency and the list ballot papers. Although they were operating under a more proportional system, it appeared that the parties were fighting the campaign on rather traditional tactics. Most of the media coverage also tended towards a traditional approach. The main focus was on the party leaders and speculation about possible coalitions between the parties in the event that no overall majority was achieved. This left little room for coverage of the smaller parties and independent candidates, nor for a more imaginative coverage of the impact of a more proportional electoral system.

Two incidents were to add a little colour, both featuring the leader of the SNP, Alex Salmond. The first was domestic, the second international. The SNP had already indicated its intention to levy additional taxes to meet its manifesto commitments should it be elected, but the issue became more controversial following the

17

Budget from the Chancellor, Gordon Brown, in March 1999 and his announcement that the basic rate of income tax would be cut by 1p. The response of the SNP was to commit themselves to invoke the parliament's tax-varying powers to reinstate the penny in the pound, using the revenue to improve public services. But the move backfired somewhat when, under pressure from the media, Salmond's detailed plans for spending the extra revenue were less forthcoming. More hostile media attention followed Salmond's controversial statement over the British government's role in Kosovo, referring to the NATO bombing as an 'unpardonable folly'. Questions were asked about whether the Nationalists, and in particular their leader, had committed two key electoral blunders – the first to promise to raise taxation and the other to speak out against the government during a war (Jones 1999). On the other hand, it did give the SNP a voice on an international issue that dominated media coverage throughout the election campaign. What is more, the SNP slippage in the polls occurred long before the campaign started, and despite a further drop in the middle, they finished at much the same level where they had begun in early March (McCrone 1999).

THE HISTORIC ELECTION

Mist and rain covered most of Scotland on 6 May 1999, not ideal conditions for an election, and constitutional campaigners were anxious that the weather would have a negative impact on turnout figures. As the results came through and were announced in the early hours of the next morning, it became clear that, as expected, no party would have an overall majority of seats in the parliament. Just 59 per cent of the electorate turned out to cast their vote, substantially short of the 71 per cent who voted in the 1997 Westminster election (but much the same as in the referendum, and as in elections to home-rule parliaments elsewhere in Europe, such as in Catalonia). As the results were analysed, it was evident that some voters had not simply voted in the same way as they would have done for a Westminster election; further, some voters had indeed voted differently on the constituency and regional ballots. The decisions of those who did vote differently made a difference (a point which we analyse further in Chapter 3, especially in Table 3.1, and in Chapter 5). Labour still benefited from the first-past-the-post constituency votes, but with fifty-six seats in total, it was far short of a majority. Neither did the SNP achieve the breakthrough some had hoped for, although it confirmed its place as the main challenge to Labour, gaining thirty-five seats with slightly under 30 per cent of the vote. There was some disappointment for the Liberal Democrats, too, who were one of the main advocates of electoral reform. Under the new system the party obtained just seventeen seats, coming behind the Conservative Party with eighteen seats. It was particularly ironic for some that the Conservatives should gain significant representation in a parliament they had campaigned against and with an electoral system they opposed. Smaller parties also benefited, with the Scottish Green Party and the Scottish Socialist Party gaining one seat each. The remaining constituency seat was won by Dennis Canavan, much to the embarrassment of the Scottish Labour Party leadership but to the pleasure of his supporters and to critics of Labour's selection process (see Table 2.1).

Table 2.1 Scottish Parliament election results

| Party | Constituency vote % | Regional vote % | No. of seats | | | |
			Const.	Reg.	Total	%
Conservative	15.5	15.4	0	18	18	14
Labour	38.8	33.6	53	3	56	43
Liberal Democrat	14.2	12.4	12	5	17	13
SNP	28.7	27.3	7	28	35	27
Others*	2.7	11.3	1	2	3	2
Totals			73	56	129	

* One Independent Labour (constituency seat), one Scottish Socialist Party and one Scottish Green Party (both regional seats)

The pressure to get more women into the parliament also paid dividends. All records for women's representation in Scotland were broken when forty-eight women were elected (see Table 2.2), making up 37 per cent of the members of the new Parliament. Labour's 'twinning' mechanism resulted in exactly the same number of male and female MSPs, the 50:50 for which women activists had campaigned during the years of the Convention. The SNP's approach of placing women high on the party lists helped return fifteen women

MSPs, some 43 per cent of their total representation. Without any mechanism or special measures the Conservatives and the Liberal Democrats lagged well behind.

Table 2.2 Gender composition of the Scottish Parliament

Party	Elected MSPs (number)		Elected MSPs (% women)
	Women	Men	
Conservative	3	15	17
Labour	28	28	50
Liberal Democrat	2	15	12
SNP	15	20	43
Others*	0	3	0
Totals	48	81	37

* Includes two male representatives from the Scottish Socialist Party and the Scottish Green Party and one male Independent MSP

ANALYSING THE RESULTS

Full analyses of the results of the first elections to the Scottish Parliament, based on the Scottish Parliamentary Election Study, are explored in the chapters that follow. Initial observations highlight some key features already identified, including turnout, the extent of ticket-splitting, the level of proportionality and representation achieved under the new electoral system, and comparison with the 1997 election for Westminster seats.

As noted, the turnout was less than the 1997 Westminster election but somewhat higher than usual turnout for local elections. The average of 58.8 per cent hid considerable variation across Scotland. The Labour stronghold of Glasgow recorded the lowest at 47.5 per cent while Dunbartonshire was the highest at 64.3 per cent (Denver and McAllister 1999: Table 10). Turnout varied according to the level of competition for parliamentary seats and social and economic indicators. In general, it was higher in seats that were more marginal in the 1997 general election, in more middle-class areas, in con-stituencies where there were more owner-occupiers, and in rural areas. In contrast, turnouts were lower in more socially deprived urban areas and in constituencies with a greater percentage of young people and ethnic minority communities.

As Table 2.1 illustrates, all of the main political parties attracted less support in the regional list vote than they enjoyed in the constituency ballots. Support for the Scottish Labour Party fell by over 5 per cent from 38.8 per cent of the constituency votes to 33.6 per cent of the list votes. Perhaps more surprisingly, support for the Scottish Liberal Democrats fell from 14.2 per cent in the constituency to 12.4 per cent in the list votes, while both the SNP and the Conservatives also failed to attract a higher percentage of votes on the party lists. The main beneficiaries were the smaller parties and independent candidates, support for whom rose from 2.7 per cent in the constituency votes to 11.3 per cent in the list votes. However, as Denver and McAllister (1999) note, the net effects of movement between parties make precise calculation of the extent of ticket-splitting much more problematic. With almost all electors using both of their votes, there was little evidence of the predicted confusion amongst voters that dominated much of the media coverage of the election campaign. We analyse the ways in which people split their votes in much greater detail in Chapter 5.

If one of the objectives of the new system was to ensure that there was a closer relationship between the votes received for a political party and the seats they obtained in the parliament, then this was clearly achieved, as can be seen by comparing Table 2.1 with Table 2.3 (which shows the results in the Scottish seats in the 1997 UK general election). However, as the figures in Table 2.1 show, the system did not provide a totally proportional result. Labour's advantage in the first-past-the-post constituency seats meant that they achieved 43 per cent of the total seats with an average of 36 per cent of the vote. The relationship between the votes cast and seats gained for the other main parties shows a closer correlation, but it is the smaller parties and independent candidates who benefit least from the form of AMS adopted.

Table 2.2 provides evidence of greater social representativeness of elected members, at least as far as gender is concerned. But the selection processes of the parties and the new electoral system failed to return any non-white MSPs, a factor that is likely to influence future policy to redress the situation.

Table 2.3 Scottish results in UK election 1997

Party	Vote	Seats	
	%	No.	%
Conservative	17.5	0	0
Labour	45.6	56	78
Liberal Democrat	13.0	10	14
SNP	22.1	6	8
Others	1.9	0	0
Totals		72	

A topic which attracted attention before the elections for the Scottish Parliament was the extent to which people would vote differently from the way they had cast their votes for the Westminster elections in 1997. It was expected, for example, that support for the SNP would increase on the grounds that there was much more point in voting for the party under a proportional system for Scottish elections. The Scottish Labour Party was expected to be the main casualty of a shift in vote towards the nationalists (Brown *et al.* 1998, 1999). By comparing Tables 2.1 and 2.3, we can see that support for the Scottish Labour Party fell from 45.6 per cent in 1997 to 38.8 per cent in 1999. The Conservatives also saw a further decline in their electoral support from 17.5 per cent to 15.5 per cent, but without the devastating seat loss that occurred in 1997. A rise in support for the SNP is evident, from 22.1 per cent for Westminster to 28.7 per cent for the Scottish elections, although they failed to break through the 30 per cent that many had expected. Comparison between the results of the two elections also shows a rise in support for the Scottish Liberal Democrats from 13 per cent in 1997 to 14.2 per cent in 1999, with the smaller parties showing an increase from 1.9 per cent to 2.7 per cent. The main shift to note from the perspective of the smaller parties is, of course, the rise of their vote to 11.3 per cent for the regional seats. These shifts of vote are analysed in more detail later in the book, especially in Chapters 3, 5 and 8.

AFTER THE ELECTION

With the election over, there was no time for rest, as preparations were made for the first meeting of the Parliament on 12 May, and minds turned to which party or parties would form the government. The most likely outcome was a coalition between Labour and the Liberal Democrats, the two main parties in the Scottish Constitutional Convention. Other coalition partnerships were deemed unlikely. However, the possibility of Labour forming a minority government was taken more seriously. Following a few days of uncertainty, Labour and the Liberal Democrats finally announced their partnership for government on 14 May, producing a document entitled *Partnership Scotland* (Finnie and McLeish 1999). As expected, Donald Dewar, the leader of the Labour Party, was elected by the parliament as its First Minister, and he in turn appointed Jim Wallace, leader of the Liberal Democrats, as his Depute. Donald Dewar appointed eleven Cabinet Ministers (nine Labour and two Liberal Democrats) who are supported by a further eleven Junior Ministers (nine Labour and two Liberal Democrats). The Scotland Act refers to the Scottish government as the Scottish 'Executive', a matter of some controversy among people – mainly nationalists – who claimed that this demeaned the status of the Parliament. The title is also confusing because it refers to both the political executive (the ministers) and the civil servants who staff the government departments.

A legislative programme covering eight bills was announced which proposed reforms for education, transport, land tenure, the feudal system, national parks, local government, disabled adults and finance and auditing. The first real test for the coalition came on the question of tuition fees for students in higher education (see Chapter 9). A potential split over the issue emerged as members of the Liberal Democrats opposed Labour's policy and restated their pre-election promise to abolish fees. They were supported in this stance by the other non-Executive parties. Labour avoided a damaging vote on the issue by setting up a Committee of Inquiry into student finance, chaired by Andrew Cubie. When the Committee reported at the end of 1999 it made recommendations which attracted wide support. Although these recommendations were not fully endorsed by Labour, a settlement between the coalition partners was reached which went some way to meet the objections raised by their opponents, and a crisis was averted.

This potential area of conflict presented a number of difficulties for the coalition so early in the life of the Parliament, and for the new type of politics that had been heralded. Before the election, a view was articulated across the political parties and in Scottish civil society that the Scottish Parliament should operate differently from the Westminster model. The adoption of a more proportional electoral system and the election of more women MSPs was part of this difference. To help engender a more collaborative political culture, and one that could be distinguished from the Westminster model, the cross-party Consultative Steering Group charged with drafting Standing Orders and Procedures for the Parliament had endorsed four key principles: power-sharing, accountability, access and participation, and equal opportunities. It proposed ways in which the Parliament should be run and conduct its affairs and recommended a powerful role for parliamentary committees to extend beyond scrutinising the work of the executive with a view to allowing them to contribute to the development of policy and even initiate their own legislation. Their role in influencing the pre-legislative process was highlighted and they were encouraged to enhance participation in the policy process by drawing on expertise and advice from different sources, holding inquiries where necessary, and holding their meetings in different parts of Scotland.

Sixteen committees were established in 1999, eight covering statutory functions (Audit; Equal Opportunities; Europe; Finance; Procedures; Public Petitions; Standards; Subordinate Legislation) and eight covering specific subjects (Education, Culture and Sport; Enterprise and Lifelong Learning; Health and Community Care; Local Government; Justice and Home Affairs; Rural Affairs; Housing and the Voluntary Sector; Transport and the Environment). It was intended that they should have cross-cutting functions in order for linkages between different policy areas to be drawn. The composition of committees reflects the composition of the Parliament itself: that is, no party has an overall majority, and not all of the committees are chaired by MSPs from the governing coalition.

But the early days of the Parliament did not exactly live up to the expectations of a different type of politics, with damaging disputes over members' pay and allowances. Old political habits have proved hard to break. A more co-operative spirit was evident on 1 July 1999 when the Parliament was officially opened by the Queen and the formal transfer of powers took place. The new First Minister, Donald Dewar, spoke of a 'new life for Scotland and all of her people', and his sentiments were endorsed by the Depute First Minister, Jim

Wallace, who stated that 'it must be our responsibility as members of the Scottish Parliament to make the Parliament succeed for all of Scotland – for the whole of our nation' and by Alex Salmond, leader of the SNP, who pledged that 'all our efforts will be on their [the Scottish people's] behalf'. Although his party was initially opposed to the Parliament, the leader of the Scottish Conservatives, David McLetchie, said that they were 'totally committed to making this Parliament work successfully for Scotland in a renewed partnership within the United Kingdom' (*The Scotsman* 2 July 1999).

In spite of this display of common purpose, it is not surprising that old party rivalries continue to exist and are played out in the parliamentary chamber, although a more co-operative atmosphere is evident in parliamentary committees. Even at the beginning of its second year of operation, the new parliament is still finding its feet and the parliamentary committees are learning as they experiment with different ways of operating. Although the coalition survived the first test over tuition fees, the Executive has had to face other challenges during the short life of the Parliament. For example, in autumn 2000, the Executive was under pressure in the wake of what was arguably the biggest crisis ever to hit Scottish education, the failure of the examination system managed by the Scottish Qualifications Agency. The Education Committee and the Lifelong Learning Committee were given the momentous task of enquiring into what Donald Dewar called a 'disaster', and of drawing broad lessons for how public policy should be made (Paterson 2000d).

CONCLUSION

The first election to the Scottish Parliament have indeed proved to be a significant turning-point for politics in Scotland. Scotland's four-party system has grown to include representatives from the small parties; the SNP has been confirmed as the main opposition to the Labour Party; the hegemony that Labour has enjoyed in Scottish elections has been dented; there is a 'critical mass' of women politicians in the new chamber; and Scotland is experiencing the challenges and uncertainties of coalition government. In addition, voters in Scotland have demonstrated their willingness to vote differently in elections for Westminster and for the Edinburgh parliament. The Parliament is also learning to operate under rules and procedures that are significantly different from the Westminster model. The precise consequences of all these changes for the nature of party competition, the role of individual MSPs and the process of government have yet to be fully realised.

This chapter has set the scene and the political context in which the first election for the Scottish Parliament can be fully understood. It has discussed the way in which acceptance of a scheme for a Scottish Parliament developed over the previous twenty years and gained wide acceptance in Scottish political life. Even if that acceptance remained largely at the level of a political élite, it helped influence the legitimacy and acceptability of Labour's proposals in 1997. The debates about constitutional options and the prospects for a Scottish Parliament were played out extensively during the Westminster election in 1997 and the referendum that followed in the same year, a factor that no doubt had an impact on the campaign and turnout for the historic election in 1999. But it is to these and other questions that the rest of this book now turns. The following chapters deal with the issues raised in this one in more detail, drawing conclusions and lessons that are of significance for all the political players in the new Scotland.

NOTES

1   This chapter is informed by an earlier article – see Brown 1999.

3

MAY 6 1999: AN ELECTION IN SCOTLAND OR A SCOTTISH ELECTION?

—•~~ΛΛΛRρ⊚ΛRΛΛ~•—

INTRODUCTION

The election held on 6 May 1999 determined the composition of the first Scottish Parliament to be assembled for nearly 300 years. But it was far from being Scotland's first taste of devolution. Not only had the Treaty of Union preserved the country's separate legal system, but since 1885 it had also enjoyed its own department of state (Kellas 1989). The 1999 election simply heralded the transformation of devolution, not its birth. The former system of administrative devolution was replaced by a new one of legislative devolution. The job of the new parliament was primarily to take over from Westminster responsibility for legislating in those policy areas that had previously come under the purview of the Scottish Office (Scottish Office 1997).

The transformation may not have been new but it was radical. Under administrative devolution, the question of who ran the Scottish Office was determined by the outcome of UK general elections. Equally, Scottish legislation had to secure the approval of the UK-wide Westminster parliament. In contrast, under legislative devolution, who runs the Scottish Executive is determined by the outcome of a

27

Scotland-only election and Scottish legislation needs only the approval of MSPs sitting in Holyrood. In short, the introduction of legislative devolution decisively shifted the source of authority in domestic Scottish politics.

The rationale behind this change was of course simple. While it was always possible under administrative devolution for different public policies to be pursued in Scotland and in England, the likelihood that it would happen was always constrained by the tendency for single-party UK governments to want to pursue a coherent policy (Brown *et al.* 1998; Kellas 1989; Paterson 1994). In contrast, under legislative devolution a Scottish government would have the freedom to pursue whatever policy it thought was best irrespective of whatever the UK government thought. 'Scottish solutions for Scottish problems' became the rhetorical cry of pro-devolution campaigners.

But there is a crucial assumption behind this argument. This is that Scottish elections will indeed lend the Scottish Parliament and Executive an authority that is independent of that of Westminster. But whether they do or not will depend on the motivations that voters bring to the ballot box in devolved elections.

Perhaps voters will vote in devolved elections on the basis of those issues that confront the Scottish Parliament, ignoring whatever may be going on at Westminster. As a result, they might, for example, be prepared to vote Labour in a Scottish election even though the party is unpopular at Westminster. If this is what happens, then whoever wins power in Scotland can claim to owe their election to their own popularity and not to the popularity of the parties at Westminster. In these circumstances we would expect that the Scottish Parliament and Executive would feel willing and able to pursue their own policy direction even if that direction met with hostility from Westminster.

On the other hand, Westminster might loom larger than this in voters' minds. Perhaps because they see what is going at Westminster as more important than what happens at Holyrood, voters might regard a Scottish election as an opportunity to express their feelings about the current performance of the parties at Westminster. As a result they might in fact, for example, be prepared to vote Labour in a Scottish election only if they are happy with the performance of Labour at a UK level. In these circumstances it would be difficult indeed for whoever wins power in Edinburgh to claim a mandate that is truly independent of Westminster. And we would expect that the Scottish Parliament would be less inclined to pursue its own policy agenda, and certainly that it would be less able to maintain a particular course of action in the face of hostility from Westminster.

If the Scottish Parliament is to be a body that pursues 'Scottish solutions for Scottish problems' then it needs the Scottish electorate to be willing to give 'Scottish answers to Scottish questions'. Yet few students of either European or local elections would argue that this is something to be taken for granted. It has long been accepted that, for the most part, voters regard European elections as an opportunity to express a judgement on the merits of their current national government. As a result, European elections have done little to enhance the status and authority of the European parliament, let alone helped to instil into the voters of Europe any sense of pan-European identity (van der Eijk and Franklin 1996). Meanwhile, although voters do appear to have some regard for the performance of their local council in deciding how to vote in local elections, it is also evident that across the UK as a whole the fortunes of the parties in local elections are heavily influenced by the current popularity of the parties at Westminster (Miller 1988; Heath *et al.* 1999; Rallings and Thrasher 1997).

This feature of European and local elections has resulted in their being dubbed 'second-order' elections (Reif and Schmitt 1980; Reif 1984). In such elections voters are none too bothered about the institution for which they are voting. As a result, turnout tends to be relatively low. But even those who do turn out to vote do not necessarily vote about the issues that are supposedly at stake in the election. Rather they vote on the basis of what has been happening in what they consider to be a more important institution, such as the national government. In other words, voters use a second-order election to express their views about the performance of the incumbent national government to date. In so doing, they may even act strategically, voting against the government in order to express some discontent even though they might well be prepared to vote to re-elect that government in a general election. After all, in a second-order election one can vote for an opposition party safe in the knowledge that there is no chance that it will actually form the government. Indeed this might well be one reason why, in a second-order election, voters are also more inclined to support a smaller party; such parties can be given encouragement without fear that they will win power. In any case, given that the election does not matter so much, voters might well reason that they could afford to risk backing a small party whose ideas they might like but whose electoral prospects appear dim.

There are then three symptoms of a second order election – low turnout, a decline in support for the incumbent government party, and higher support for minor parties. And as we can see from Chapter 2, all three of these symptoms were evident in the first Scottish election. There does then seem good reason to inquire further whether the outcome of the first Scottish election was consistent with the hopes and aspirations of the framers of devolution.

That is the task of this chapter. In particular we concentrate on why Labour's vote was apparently so low. (What we might learn from the low turnout is discussed later, in Chapter 4.) Was this decline a reaction to the performance of the UK government, rendering the first Scottish election no more than just another election in Scotland? Or was the decline made in Scotland, with the implication that the election was truly a Scottish event? On ascertaining the answers to these questions we consider the implications both for the future of devolution and also for the theory of first and second order elections.

LABOUR'S LOSSES: MADE IN SCOTLAND
OR MADE IN BRITAIN?

Certainly, if we ask voters themselves why they voted the way that they did, then it would appear that for the majority it was developments in Scotland alone that were at the forefront of their minds. Just over half said that they decided how they would vote on the basis of what was going on in Scotland, while just under a third said that they primarily took into account what was happening in Britain as a whole. This appears to suggest the outcome of the first Scottish election was indeed made in Scotland.

Other information also helps to corroborate this story. If voters were voting differently from the way they would have done in a Westminster election, then we would expect that they would be more likely to say that they decided how they would vote close to polling day than has been the case in recent Westminster elections.

After all, this was the first occasion on which voters had had the chance to vote in a Scottish election. So, if they were making a different decision from the one they had previously made in a Westminster election, then more of them should have been making a fresh choice and fewer simply expressing old loyalties. And indeed our expectation is fulfilled. Nearly a half of Scots said that they decided how to vote in the Scottish election either during the campaign or else no earlier than the year of the election. By contrast, only just over a third gave such an answer after the 1997 general election.

This does not, however, seem to have stopped most voters voting in exactly the same way as they said they would have done if it had been a Westminster election that had been held on 6 May 1999. On the constituency vote no fewer than 82 per cent said they voted in the same way as they said they would have done in a Westminster election. On the regional vote the figure falls only somewhat to 76 per cent. Moreover the degree of correspondence (on the constituency vote) was only six points lower among those who said that they voted primarily on the basis of what was going on in Scotland than it was among those who said that they voted on the basis of what was going on in Britain as a whole. Perhaps those in the former group who voted the same way decided to support the same party for different reasons from those they would have applied in a Westminster election. But perhaps also we should not assume that those who said they were voting on the basis of what was going on in Scotland were in fact ignoring the record of the UK Labour government in the previous two years in deciding how to vote.

Moreover, on both Holyrood ballots, more people voted in the same way as they would have done in a Westminster election than did so in the local elections that were held the same day as the first Scottish election. Here only 71 per cent voted the same way as they would have done in a Westminster election. While the latter figure may in part at least be accounted for by voting in local elections for independent candidates, candidates who for the most part are absent from Westminster and Holyrood elections but are still prominent in local elections in rural Scotland (Bochel and Denver 1999), we certainly do not have any convincing evidence here that Scottish elections are less likely to be influenced by Westminster considerations than are local ones.

31

Yet arguably what matters in ensuring that the politicians of Holyrood have a mandate independent from that of their counterparts at Westminster is not how many people vote differently in a Scottish election from the way they would have done in a Westminster one, but rather whether the decisions of those who do vote differently have any impact on the outcome. Even if a relatively large proportion of voters had voted differently in the first Scottish election from their Westminster preference, we might conclude that this did little to give the Scottish Parliament a separate mandate if the various decisions of these voters had no net impact on the outcome. On the other hand, we might come to the opposite view if the decisions of those who did vote differently had a discernible impact on the result, even if this group clearly constitutes only a minority.

Table 3.1 Distribution of reported vote

Party	Holyrood first preference	Westminster hypothetical Vote	Difference
	%	%	%
Conservative	16	16	0
Labour	39	48	−9
Liberal Democrat	15	14	+1
SNP	28	21	+7
Sample size (=100%)	1,060	1,239	

Those who did not vote in the Scottish election and those who said they would not vote in a Westminster election are excluded from the relevant column, as are those who for some other reason failed to name a party.
Source: Scottish Parliamentary Election Survey 1999

Table 3.1 suggests that the behaviour of the one in five or so who did vote differently from their Westminster preference did indeed have an impact. To simplify matters somewhat, instead of looking at either the distribution of the constituency or the regional vote in the Scottish election, and debating which – if either – represented voters' real preference in the Scottish election, we look at how people said they would have voted if they had simply been asked to express a first preference. As it happens, the distribution of support on this measure is closer to that of the constituency vote than it is to that of the regional vote. But what matters to us here is that it is very different from the distribution of support in a hypothetical Westminster election. Labour's support was no fewer than nine points lower in the Scottish election than it would have been in a Westminster election held at the same time. Meanwhile, the SNP's vote was no fewer than seven points higher. It looks as though the first Scottish election was indeed no simple replica of a Westminster election.

True, we should bear in mind that part of the difference between the two outcomes reflects the impact of differential turnout rather than vote switching. We asked all of our respondents how they would have voted in a Westminster election, not just those who voted in the Scottish election. And more of those who said they would vote Labour in a Westminster election failed to participate in the Holyrood election than did of those who said they would vote for any of the other parties. As Table 3.2 shows, no fewer than one in four of Labour's potential supporters stayed at home, compared with just under one in five potential Conservative voters and fewer than one in six SNP or Liberal Democrat supporters. But even if we limit the comparison in Table 3.1 to those who did vote in the Scottish election, we still find that Labour were seven points adrift of their Westminster tally while the SNP were six points higher. That switching from Labour to the SNP was indeed a key reason for Labour's 'underperformance' can be seen from the fact that in Table 3.2 more Westminster Labour supporters (7 per cent) switched to the SNP than switched to all of the other parties combined (6 per cent).

Table 3.2 How Westminster support was retained and lost

	Voted in Scottish Parliament Election for:						
Would have voted in UK General Election for:	Con	Lab	Lib Dem	SNP	Other	Did Not Vote	sample size (=100%)
Conservative	71	2	4	4	*	19	193
Labour	1	62	3	7	2	25	598
Liberal Democrat	5	5	63	11	1	16	167
SNP	2	2	1	76	3	16	255
Would Not Vote	2	5	3	8	1	80	170

* less than 1
Source: Scottish Parliamentary Election Survey 1999

Yet we should be careful before we jump to the conclusion that these differences between the Holyrood and Westminster outcomes mean that the first Scottish election was not a second-order election. The theory of second-order elections does not simply argue that voters behave in such elections in exactly the same way as they would do in a first-order election. Rather, as we noted at the beginning, it suggests that a second-order election is a chance to protest about the behaviour of the incumbent government without having to worry that an anti-government swing will enable the opposition to win power. In short, parties of government, as Labour was in 1999, will often do less well in a second-order election than they would have done in a first-order election held at the same time. The difference between Labour's Westminster and Scottish support as revealed in Table 3.1 could well then be wholly consistent with the first Scottish election simply being a second-order election. To establish whether or not Labour's shortfall in the Scottish election represents a protest vote against the UK Labour government or is in fact a reflection of Labour's standing in the eyes of the electorate on matters closer to home, we have to analyse the reasons why some voters who would have backed Labour in a Westminster election failed to do so in the first Scottish election.

Table 3.3 Perceptions of the UK government record

| | % saying got better minus % saying got worse since 1997 election: | |
	among all voters	among Labour Westminster 'voters'
Unemployment	+7	+15
Living standards	+6	+17
Education	+3	+17
National Health Service	−11	+3
Taxes	−29	−8
Sample size	1,482	598

Source: Scottish Parliamentary Election Survey 1999

Our first step in that task is to look at what Scots voters made of the UK Labour government's record in its first two years in office. In truth, Table 3.3 hardly suggests an electorate that was motivated to protest about the record of the incumbent UK government. Among

Scots as a whole, slightly more thought that unemployment had fallen since the general election than thought it had risen. Equally, more thought that general living standards and the quality of education in schools had gone up than thought they had gone down. Only on health and taxes is there any evidence of dissatisfaction (that is, more people thought that taxes had gone up than thought they had gone down). Moreover when we look at those who say they would have voted Labour in a general election, the government's ratings are even higher.

But whatever the distribution of satisfaction and dissatisfaction with the party's record at Westminster, there is no evidence at all that, among those who said they would vote Labour in a general election, expressing dissatisfaction on a particular issue made it less likely that they would name Labour as their first preference party in the Scottish election. Rather, as Table 3.4 shows, what is remarkable is the almost complete absence of any relationship among hypothetical Labour Westminster supporters between evaluations of the Labour government's record and propensity to fail to back the party for the Scottish election.[1] Thus, for example, while just over one in three of those who thought that unemployment had gone up failed to back Labour for the Scottish election, so also did just over one in three of those who thought that unemployment had fallen. In short, thinking that Labour had a good record in office failed to act as a barrier to defection in the Scottish election.[2]

Table 3.4 Perceptions of UK government's record and Labour defection

	% Labour Westminster voters not preferring Labour in Scottish elections among those whose evaluation of government record was:			
	Favourable	*sample size (=100%)*	*Unfavourable*	*sample size (=100%)*
Unemployment	35	260	36	166
Living standards	37	223	40	120
Education	37	203	35	110
National Health Service	39	193	37	238
Taxes	39	161	37	238

Source: Scottish Parliamentary Election Survey 1999

So here we have what appears to be decisive evidence that the first

Scottish election was not simply a second-order election. Labour may have lost votes but it did not do so on account of the public's evaluation of its record at Westminster. Evidently its electoral difficulties were created rather closer to home.

But does this mean that voters were in fact giving Scottish answers to Scottish questions? Can we demonstrate that voters failed to back Labour because they were unhappy about some of its policy proposals for the new parliament? Or perhaps they were simply less keen on the party's Scottish leader, Donald Dewar, than they were on its UK leader, Tony Blair? If so then we will have shown not only that what was going on at Westminster did not matter, but also that voters were indeed voting on the basis of the issues that were confronting the new institution for which they were being asked to vote.

As noted in Chapter 2, two issues dominated the first Scottish election campaign: tuition fees for university students and the SNP's proposal to put a penny on income tax. On neither of these two issues were Labour's stances particularly popular with those who said that they would back the party in a UK general election. As Table 3.5 shows, nearly two out of three said that if there had to be a choice they would rather have higher taxes and higher spending on health or education than leave taxes and spending as they were (or indeed lowering both). Meanwhile, although a half said that they favoured the current Labour policy on tuition fees, which entailed some students having to pay tuition fees depending on their circumstances, over two in five said that they favoured abolition. (The tuition fees issue itself is analysed in more detail in Chapter 9.) If those who disagreed with Labour on these issues did defect as a result, there would certainly seem to be enough of them to account for the scale of the support Labour lost in the Scottish election.

Table 3.5 Support for Labour's stance on Scottish issues

	% Labour Westminster voters who	
	Support party policy	Oppose party policy
Tuition fees	52	42
Increase tax for education	36	61
Increase tax for health	35	63

Sample size 598
Source: Scottish Parliamentary Election Survey 1999

Yet when we look, as we do in Table 3.6, at what those Westminster Labour voters who disagreed with their party's policy on these two issues actually did in the Scottish election, we find little evidence that they were particularly inclined to defect. True there are some small differences. Thus, for example, among those who opposed the party's policy on tuition fees, 42 per cent failed to back the party, while the equivalent figure among those who supported tuition fees was 35 per cent. But this seven-point gap and the similar gaps on taxation and spending are hardly able to account for more than a small fraction of Labour's loss of support. So while the performance of the UK government does not appear to have had much impact on the Scottish electorate, neither also do the issues that apparently faced the new parliament.

Table 3.6 Scottish issues and Labour defection

| | % Labour Westminster voters not preferring Labour in Scottish elections among those who | |
	Support party policy	Oppose party policy
Tuition fees	35	42
Increase tax for education	35	41
Increase tax for health	36	40

Sample size 598
Source: Scottish Parliamentary Election Survey 1999

There is one area where a purely Holyrood question did have an impact. This was voters' evaluation of Donald Dewar. Among those Westminster Labour supporters who did not think that Donald Dewar would make the best First Minister, as many as 54 per cent defected. In contrast only 34 per cent of those who thought he would make the best First Minister failed to back the party in the Scottish election. But we should bear in mind that the vast majority of Labour supporters were in the latter camp. Unsurprisingly, 78 per cent of them thought that Donald Dewar would make the best First Minister. So in practice even this more substantial difference in defection rates does little to account for the party's overall electoral performance.

It appears then that we can find little evidence to support either a claim that the first Scottish election was a first-order event or that it was a second-order occasion. Evidently we need to question the utility of the lens through which we have been looking so far. It certainly seems to ignore one important possibility. This is that, rather than being an election about either Westminster or Holyrood, the first Scottish election was about the relationship between the two. Some scholars have indeed argued that rather than simply being second-order events European elections are in part about the relationship between a member country and the rest of the Union (Curtice and Steed 2000). Perhaps we should ask whether the first Scottish election was yet another stage in the long-running debate about Scotland's position in the Union.

Such debate was hardly absent from the election campaign (see also Chapter 2). In theory Scotland's constitutional position is a matter reserved for Westminster to decide and so cannot be affected by the outcome of a Holyrood election. Yet using the slogan, 'divorce is an expensive business', the Labour Party made attacks on the SNP's policy of independence a key part of their campaign. Meanwhile the SNP leader, Alex Salmond, caused the greatest controversy of all by criticising in a television broadcast NATO's decision to bomb Serbia and Kosovo. His claim that it was 'unpardonable folly' was a dramatic illustration of his party's belief that an independent Scotland would be capable of pursuing a different foreign policy from England.

Perhaps, then, these are the issues that account for the difference between Labour's potential level of support in a Westminster election and the support it was able to realise in the first Scottish election. In electing a Scottish Parliament, voters may have been looking for those politicians who they thought would best promote Scotland's interests *vis-à-vis* the rest of the United Kingdom – including, not least, those on subjects which, while they might lie outside Holyrood's formal powers, were ones where the new institution could be expected to advocate Scotland's cause. Holyrood may not have been viewed as powerful in its own right, as required by a theory of first-order elections, but it could still be viewed as an institution with potential influence *vis-à-vis* the other major force in the land, Westminster.

So was Labour's problem that, while it was regarded as capable of forming an effective UK government, Scots had doubts about its ability to promote Scotland's interests through the new parliament? The evidence in Table 3.7 certainly does not immediately suggest that there was a high level of concern about Scotland's position within the Union among Westminster Labour supporters. While one in three of these felt that England gets more out of the Union than does Scotland, well over half either believed that Scotland does best or that both countries do equally well. Meanwhile only one in five believed that Scotland should become independent.

Table 3.7 Views on Scotland's place in the Union

	% of Westminster Labour voters who take	
	Pro-Unionist view	Anti-Unionist view
Independence	76	21
England/Scotland benefits more from the Union	58	35

Sample size 598

Source: Scottish Parliamentary Election Survey 1999

Still, as Table 3.8 overleaf indicates, those who backed independence were far more likely to fail to back Labour in the Scottish election than were those who preferred Scotland to remain in the Union. Over half of the pro-independence group defected, compared with just one-third of backers of the Union. On the other hand, perceptions of whether England or Scotland benefited more from the Union made little apparent difference to Westminster Labour supporters' willingness to support the party in the Holyrood election.

But two other indicators of people's views on Scotland's position in the Union provide rather firmer evidence for our supposition. The first of these is Alex Salmond's decision to criticise the NATO bombing of Serbia and Kosovo. In our survey we asked our respondents not whether they thought the NATO bombing was right or wrong, but rather whether, irrespective of their own views on the bombing, Alex Salmond was right or wrong to express his doubts. While doubtless some people's answers to this question were influenced by what they thought of Mr Salmond more generally whereas others may simply have believed in a right to free speech, willingness to endorse Mr Salmond's expression of his views may also be indicative of a willingness to accept that Scotland might have a foreign policy different from that of the rest of the UK.

Despite widespread condemnation by Labour ministers of Mr Salmond's decision to speak out, no less than half of Westminster

Labour supporters felt that he was right to do so; only 44 per cent thought he was wrong. And the former group were also markedly more likely to fail to back Labour in the Scottish election. As many as 48 per cent of those who thought Mr Salmond was right to speak out failed to back Labour, while only 28 per cent of those who thought he was wrong did so.

Table 3.8 Scotland's place in the Union and Labour defection

	% of Westminster Labour voters not preferring Labour in Scottish election among those who hold a	
	Pro-Unionist view	Anti-Unionist view
Independence	34	52
England/Scotland benefits more from the Union	37	40

Sample size 598
Source: Scottish Parliamentary Election Survey 1999

The second indicator is how much trust voters have in the UK government's willingness and ability to work in Scotland's best long-term interests. Even though Labour were currently running the UK government, only 39 per cent of Westminster Labour supporters felt that they could trust the UK government 'just about always' or 'most of the time'. True, only 9 per cent thought it could 'almost never' be trusted, but no fewer than 51 per cent felt they could only trust it 'some of the time'. (This measure of trust in the UK government to work for Scotland is analysed further in Chapter 6.)

And those who were doubtful about the UK government's willingness to work for Scotland were rather less likely to support Labour in the Scottish election. Among those who at most only felt able to trust the UK government 'some of the time', as many as 42 per cent failed to vote Labour in the Scottish election. By contrast, among those who felt able to trust the UK government at least 'most of the time', this figure fell to 31 per cent. Perhaps some of those who said they could not trust the UK government to work in Scotland's best interests were simply expressing dissatisfaction with the performance of the current Labour administration at Westminster. But we have already seen that, on its own, dissatisfaction with Labour's Westminster performance was not enough to discourage people from voting Labour. So it appears that what cost Labour support was a feeling among some voters that Scotland was in danger of losing out within the Union and that, by implication, they did not regard a Labour-led Scottish government as the best means of stopping that happening.

Indeed we can follow this up by looking at what happened when we asked people to say whether they trusted Labour to work in Scotland's interests. Unsurprisingly, Westminster Labour supporters are more likely to trust Labour to work in Scotland's long-term interests than they are the UK government (a difference that, however, suggests that respondents were not simply answering the earlier question on the basis of what they thought of the current Labour government at Westminster). But even so, as many as one in five said that they only trusted Labour some of the time or not at all. While two-thirds were prepared to say that the party could be trusted most of the time, only 15 per cent felt that it worked in Scotland's interests 'just about always'.

And those who did not trust Labour to work for Scotland were certainly reluctant for it to govern within Scotland. No fewer than 58 per cent of them failed to support Labour in the first Scottish election, compared with 35 per cent of those who 'mostly' trusted Labour and just 23 per cent of those who trusted the party always. We do of course have to bear in mind that, when we ask people directly about the attributes of a political party, some may respond in a way that simply rationalises a voting decision they may well have made for quite different reasons. Thus, those who did not vote Labour in the Scottish election might well have said they regarded Labour unfavourably irrespective of the question we asked them about the party. But, given also the evidence that Labour lost out among those who were concerned about how well the UK government looked after Scotland, it appears that the principal reason for Labour's 'under-performance' in the first Scottish election was that it was not thought sufficiently capable of standing up for Scotland's interests within the Union.

So far we have looked separately at our various possible explanations of why Labour lost votes in the first Scottish election. But what happens if we put them all together in a multivariate analysis? Does the story that we have told so far appear to stand up to a more rigorous statistical analysis? In fact, as we can see in Table 3.9, we find a relatively clear story that does corroborate what we have seen so far. In the table the results of two separate logistic regression models are presented (for further details about logistic regression, see the

Appendix). In both cases the analysis is confined to Westminster Labour supporters, and the dependent variable is failing to vote Labour in the Scottish election as against doing so. In the first model we include as independent variables all of the measures we have discussed individually so far bar one, that is whether Labour can be trusted to work in Scotland's interests. In the second model we include that variable as well. The first model is thus in effect a tougher test of the importance of perceptions that Labour could not be trusted to work in Scotland's interests. The second enables us to check whether any of the relationships we might find in the first model are not simply another indicator of that apparent distrust. In both cases, a positive coefficient indicates a greater propensity not to vote Labour in the Scottish election.

Those variables that prove to be significantly associated with not voting Labour are denoted in the table by asterisks. As we might expect from our discussion so far, only a select few fall into that category, and all except one of these are indicators of Scotland's place in the Union rather than of the UK government's record or of distinctively Scottish issues. Those Westminster Labour supporters who backed independence and who upheld Salmond's expression of his views on Kosovo were significantly less likely to vote Labour in the Scottish election. The same is also true in our first model of those who were distrustful of the UK government's ability to work in Scotland's interests. And while not surprisingly this last variable becomes insignificant in our second model, where we also introduce trust in Labour's willingness to work in Scotland's interests, we can see that the new variable is significantly related to not voting Labour while our other results remain robust.

Just one other indicator proves to be significant. The small group of Westminster Labour supporters who did not think that Donald Dewar would make the best First Minister were significantly less likely to back Labour in the Scottish election. Even here we might want to bear in mind that the reason why some Westminster Labour supporters might have thought that Donald Dewar would not make the best First Minister was because they thought he would not effectively defend Scotland's interests in the Union. Meanwhile, none of our evaluations of the UK government's performance in office account for failure to back Labour at all.

Table 3.9 Accounting for Labour defection

| | Westminster Labour supporters not voting Labour vs voting Labour | | | |
| | Model I | | Model II | |
	Coefficient	Standard error	Coefficient	Standard error
UK government record:				
education better	−0.13	0.22	−0.09	0.23
education worse	−0.23	0.28	−0.19	0.28
NHS better	0.18	0.24	0.23	0.24
NHS worse	0.17	0.24	0.15	0.25
standard of living up	−0.02	0.22	0.11	0.23
standard of living down	0.20	0.27	0.19	0.27
taxes up	−0.11	0.24	−0.13	0.24
taxes down	0.07	0.25	0.12	0.26
unemployment up	−0.41	0.27	−0.35	0.28
unemployment down	−0.42	0.25	−0.39	0.25
Scottish issues:				
abolish tuition fees	0.35	0.20	0.33	0.20
Dewar not best First Minister	0.75★	0.24	0.61★	0.25
increase tax for education	0.21	0.25	0.18	0.26
increase tax for health	−0.16	0.26	−0.18	0.26
Scotland in the Union:				
independence	0.63★	0.24	0.58★	0.25
anti–devolution	0.20	0.28	0.13	0.28
England benefits from Union	−0.09	0.22	−0.01	0.23
Scotland benefits from Union	0.19	0.26	0.08	0.26
Salmond right to express views on Kosovo	0.65★	0.20	0.63★	0.20
do not trust UK government to work for Scotland	0.43★	0.18	0.28	0.19
do not trust Labour to work for Scotland	–	–	0.62★	0.18

Based on 525 respondents who said they would have voted Labour in a Westminster election and for whom other measures in the model were not missing. Cell entries are logistic regression coefficients and standard errors. Except for two trust items, the coefficients compare the effect of being in the stated category rather than being in the category not included in the table for that variable (eg believing that there has been no effect of the UK government on education). The two trust variables are treated as interval level variables; the higher the score the less trusting the respondent. However, in the case of 'Do not trust UK government' those who almost never trust the government have been given the same score as those who trust it 'only some of the time'.
★statistically significant at the 5 per cent level

Source: Scottish Parliamentary Election Survey 1999

The first Scottish election was then, it seems, neither a first-order nor a second-order affair. Labour did not lose out in the first Scottish election because voters disliked its policies for the new parliament or because they were dissatisfied with the party's performance at Westminster; rather, it lost out because voters were placing more emphasis in a Scottish election than they would in a Westminster election on voting for a party that they thought would use the new institution to advance Scotland's interests within the United Kingdom. Rather than 'Whither Scotland?' or 'Whither the UK?', the question Scots were asking was 'Whither Scotland within the UK?' And it was a question to which, it seems, Labour was not always thought to be the best answer.

CONCLUSION

Relatively few voters appear to have determined their vote on the basis of issues that lay within the competence of the Holyrood parliament. But this did not mean that the hopes and aspirations of devolutionists were simply dashed. The outcome of the first Scottish election was very different from what would have happened in a Westminster election held at the same time. This was not because the election was seen as a chance to cast a risk-free protest vote against the incumbent Westminster government. Rather, voters revealed that what they are looking for in a Scottish election are parties that are willing to use the devolved institutions to promote Scotland's interests, irrespective of whether a particular decision lay within the competence of the new parliament to decide or not. Thus any Scottish government that wants to be re-elected is likely to have to demonstrate to the electorate that it has used its stewardship to advocate Scotland's interests, including taking a different stance from Westminster if necessary. If this interpretation is correct, then the new parliament may well find that it does have the public support it needs to allow it to supply, when necessary, Scottish rather than UK answers to Scottish questions.

If the expectations of devolutionists survived the test of the first Scottish election, the same cannot necessarily be said of the theory of first- and second-order elections. The first Scottish election was neither clearly first order nor was it undoubtedly second order. Rather we have discovered that the theory fails to take into account a third possibility, that what might matter to voters is what an institution can achieve by influencing others. And arguably, in an increasingly inter-dependent world in which Europe in particular is playing an ever more prominent role in British politics, even UK general elections may well come to take on more of this characteristic in future too.

NOTES

1. In this and subsequent equivalent tables in this chapter we count as 'defec-tors' not only those who turned out and voted for a different party but also those Westminster Labour supporters who abstained.
2. Of course some voters might believe that while, say, unemployment had risen, this was not the fault of the Labour government, and thus no reason not to back it. But if we repeat the analysis in Table 3.4 simply for those voters who felt that the government was responsible for the outcome we still fail to find any relationship between evaluations and defection.

4

CHANGING VOTERS:
THE SOCIAL AND IDEOLOGICAL
BASIS OF VOTING BEHAVIOUR

―――⁓⁓⁓ℛℛℙⓄℛℛ⁓⁓⁓――

INTRODUCTION

In terms of the electoral cycle the time lapse between the United Kingdom general election of 1997 and the first election to the Scottish Parliament is fairly short, a span of just two years. As changes in electoral behaviour and ideology are usually considered slow moving, we might expect changes in the voting behaviour of the Scottish electorate and the basis of party competition to be relatively minor – small fluctuations in an otherwise stable political order. However, because of the wide-ranging nature of the changes in the political system represented by the setting up of the Scottish Parliament, there are reasons to think that there may indeed have been large changes in the behaviour and attitudes of the Scottish electorate. This was the first election to a Scottish Parliament in 300 years and, as we have seen in Chapter 3, the evidence suggests that there were distinctive Scottish issues at work in the minds of the electorate when casting their votes. In addition, the election was held under a new electoral system. This means that there are two distinct catalysts for change in behaviour, over and above the fluctuations of party support we might associate with changes in the images and policies of the parties. The previous chapter began to consider the first of these catalysts – the extent to which the Scottish electorate behaved in different ways at the election to the Scottish Parliament compared to those we would have expected at a UK general election held on the same day. This chapter extends that analysis to consider changes in behaviour since the 1997 general election. The next chapter considers the second of the two catalysts – the electoral system – and considers the impact of the new system on the behaviour of voters.

As well as changes in the political and electoral systems, the election to the Scottish Parliament also provided the first large-scale test of opinion of the Labour government at Westminster. As Chapter 3 has shown, the results of the election to the Scottish Parliament were distinct from those that would have occurred had a UK general election been held on the same day. It is nevertheless unlikely that votes cast in the Scottish Parliament election were entirely free of the influence of the images of the Labour government. Scotland has, over the last four decades, seen the majority of its constituencies represented by a Labour MP, even when the Conservatives held the majority in the House of Commons. In 1997, fifty-six of the seventy-two Westminster constituencies in Scotland returned a Labour MP. It is likely that the electorate in Scotland had high expectations of a Labour government at Westminster, and the extent to which these have been met is likely to have played a role in determining how votes were cast for members of the Scottish Parliament. While it is not possible entirely to separate the influence of each of the factors of change, this chapter attempts to look at changes in behaviour between the 1997 general election and the election of May 1999, focusing on the social structural and ideological basis of the vote and how the party's images changed in the two-year period since the general election.

We look primarily at the first of the two ballots in the Scottish Parliament election – the constituency vote. An examination of the relationship between the vote in this ballot and the second ballot for the regional list members is left until Chapter 5. The chapter also uses a recall of voting behaviour at the 1997 general election[1] as the baseline from which change is assessed.

The starting point for an analysis of change between two elections is the way in which supporters of each party in the earlier election subsequently voted the next time around. This analysis is sometimes called a 'flow of the vote' table. For the election to the Scottish Parliament, the earlier election that we are interested in is the 1997 general election to the House of Commons. Table 4.1 shows this analysis by reporting how people who voted for a given party in 1997 voted on the constituency vote in 1999.

Table 4.1 Flow of the vote, 1997–1999

| | *1997 General Election* | | | | |
	Did not vote	*Conservative*	*Labour*	*Liberal Democrat*	*SNP*
Did not vote	61	17	24	20	14
Conservative	4	61	1	2	0
Labour	13	8	55	7	4
Liberal Democrat	6	7	5	63	3
SNP	15	6	13	7	77
Other	0	1	1	0	2
Sample size (=100%)	248	210	654	114	202

1997 general election vote is based on respondents' recall of their voting behaviour.
Source: Scottish Parliamentary Election Survey 1999

Table 4.1 demonstrates a relatively high level of stability of voting behaviour (including non-voting) between 1997 and 1999. Around 60% of the electorate behaved in the same way at the two elections. However, this is lower than between the two general elections of 1992 and 1997 (Brown *et al.* 1999), despite the much smaller time gap between the elections. In particular the Labour Party appears to have been especially unsuccessful at retaining its vote, with just 55 per cent of those who voted Labour in 1997 voting for Labour on the constituency vote in 1999. In sharp contrast the SNP, Labour's main competition in these elections, retained 77 per cent of its support.

Table 4.1 also highlights the high levels of non-voting among those who had not voted in 1997; this may suggest that there is a small but significant group within the Scottish electorate who are disaffected from the political process, but it is broadly in line with the proportion of non-voters in the 1992 general election who did not vote in 1997 (Brown *et al.* 1999). Labour's support seems to have moved in two main directions. First, there is a greater tendency for those who voted Labour in 1997 to abstain from voting in the Scottish Parliament election when compared with those who voted for other parties in 1997: 24 per cent of those who voted Labour in 1997 did not turn out to vote at the election to the Scottish Parliament. Second, 13 per cent of Labour voters in 1997 turned out to vote for the SNP on the constituency vote in 1999. The relationship between votes cast for Labour and the SNP is especially interesting. The SNP are the opposition party in the Scottish Parliament and are the main competitors for Labour's vote. However, unlike elsewhere in the UK where the opposition parties offer distinctive ideological positions, the positions of the Labour Party and the SNP have, in recent years, been broadly similar, both adopting a left-of-centre set of policy positions. Thus, we would expect greater fluidity in votes between the two parties than we have traditionally seen between Labour and the Conservatives in Westminster elections, where the party of government and the opposition have adopted very different ideological and policy positions. (The ideological relationship between Labour and SNP in the minds of voters is analysed further in Chapter 8.)

From the data in Table 4.1 we can identify two key questions about the nature of changes in voting behaviour between 1997 and 1999:

- To what extent did the Scottish Parliament election see different groups within the electorate turn out to vote (and conversely decide not to vote)?
- Has the basis of competition between Labour and the SNP changed?

The Scottish Parliament election saw a relatively low level of turnout by comparison with the levels normally expected at UK general elections. At 59 per cent, turnout at this election was down 12 points on the General Election of 1997, itself noted for having had the lowest turnout of any general election since 1929. By comparison with local and European elections, turnout was clearly higher. The 1995 local elections saw a turnout of 44 per cent in Scotland, and the European election held shortly after the Scottish Parliament elections saw only 25 per cent turn out to vote. Table 4.1 suggests that differential turnout of supporters of different parties may have been a factor explaining differences between party performance in

1997 and 1999. As noted above, SNP voters in 1997 seem to have been more likely to turn out and vote in 1999 than supporters of other parties, most notably Labour. We begin by looking at the issue of turnout in the first Scottish Parliament election to assess to what extent different groups of voters within the electorate were more or less likely to vote in this election compared with the general election of 1997.

Table 4.2 looks at the proportions of different social groups who turned out to vote in 1997 and in 1999. Previous analysis of non-voting has shown that, while turnout is related to socio-economic factors in other countries (Verba and Nie 1972), in Britain the relationship between turnout and factors such as social class, housing tenure and age is modest (Swaddle and Heath 1989). However, work focusing on turnout in Scotland alone has not previously been conducted in detail. For the purposes of this analysis we are leaving aside the question of whether or not the Scottish Parliament election can be considered second order (and therefore be expected to have lower turnout, as discussed in Chapter 3); instead we are interested in the relative levels of turnout among different social groupings.

Considering the proportions of each social group who voted at the election, no simple relationship between turnout and social location exists, although some groups are more likely to turn out to vote than others. In other words, although those with an educational level of degree or above are more likely to vote than other educational groups, the propensity to vote does not vary linearly with education: it is not simply the case that the higher the level of educational qualification held the more likely is the individual to vote. Similarly, turnout and social class are related but not in a simple way. Thus, it is not the case that turnout is lower amongst those who are in less advantaged social positions, although this plays some part. The groups least likely to have voted are those from the youngest age groups, the under-34s, and those in rented accommodation.

Changes in turnout amongst the different groups are also important. While we see a decline in turnout in 1999 in practically all social groups, the size of this decline varies. Among those aged over 65 we see no decline in turnout between the two elections, remaining at the high level of 86 per cent voting. By comparison, we see the greatest decline in turnout among voters aged 25–34 where the proportion voting fell from 75 per cent in 1997 to just 55 per cent

Table 4.2 Turnout in elections by social group, 1997–1999

	1997		1999	
	Turnout (%)	Sample size (=100%)	Turnout (%)	Sample size (=100%)
Social class:				
Salariat	85	210	79	417
Routine non-manual	84	190	73	266
Petty Bourgeoisie	74	55	69	110
Manual foreman	82	71	66	96
Working class	80	292	70	455
Educational level:				
Degree	89	83	82	191
Higher education below				
degree level	85	118	74	213
A level/Highers	79	170	66	180
O level/CSE	77	231	68	332
None	82	268	73	559
Religion:				
None	76	280	66	586
Roman Catholic	81	125	74	215
Protestant	76	395	79	600
Other	76	82	66	76
Housing tenure:				
Owner	82	534	76	918
Rents: Local authority	80	245	70	395
Rents: Other	75	85	52	154
Age group:				
18–24	70	129	61	95
25–34	75	157	55	305
35–44	79	154	69	259
45–54	89	159	76	247
55–59	85	61	85	105
60–64	90	57	82	104
65+	86	156	86	356
Gender:				
Male	80	410	73	667
Female	82	473	72	815

Source: Scottish Parliamentary Election Survey 1999; Scottish Election Survey 1997

in 1999. Generally speaking the decline in turnout is greatest among
the groups who had lower levels of turnout in 1997, the effect of this

being to widen the differences among social groups. For example, the difference in turnout between the oldest age group (the over-65s) and the youngest age group (18–24) was sixteen percentage points in 1997 (86 per cent compared with 70 per cent) but had increased to 25 points in 1999 (86 per cent compared with 61 per cent). However, despite the effect of this differential change in turnout, differences between social groups are not, for the most part, large. Looking at social class we find a 9 per cent difference in turnout between the salariat (middle-class professionals) and the working class. The same 9 per cent gap is found between those with a degree level qualification and those with no educational qualifications.

The overall pattern from Table 4.2 is that while there are some differences between social groups, these are not especially large. Nor is it simply the case that turnout can be explained by position in a social hierarchy. In terms of these social characteristics, at least, there is little evidence to suggest that the basis of non-voting changed in 1999. Thus, we must look for other explanations of the decline in turnout in 1999.

It may be that the explanation for the lower turnout lies not with the social characteristics of the voters but with the political charac-teristics of the parties and the new institution. Table 4.3 looks at the perceived importance of the new parliament in comparison with the Westminster parliament for different groups of voters. Three groups of voters are considered, those who voted at both the 1997 general election and the 1999 election to the Scottish Parliament, those who voted in 1997 but did not vote in 1999, and those who did not vote in 1997 but who did vote in 1999.

Table 4.3 Participation in the Scottish election and views about institutional importance, 1997–1999

	% say Holyrood more important than Westminster	% say who wins matters a great deal/quite a lot		Sample size (=100%)
		Holyrood	Westminster	
Voted 1997 and 1999	47	65	60	940
Voted 1999, not 1997	49	54	44	93
Voted 1997, not 1999	38	43	51	255

Source: Scottish Parliamentary Election Survey 1999

We can see that those who failed to vote in the first Scottish election after having participated in the previous general election were the least likely to regard the Scottish Parliament as more important than Westminster. Thus, among those who failed to turn out for the first Scottish election but did vote in 1997, only just over one-third thought that Holyrood would have more influence than Westminster. People in this group were also more likely to say that the outcome of a Westminster election matters than they were to say the same of the outcome of a Scottish one. By contrast, among those who did participate nearly half felt that a Scottish election was more important than a Westminster one, while they were also more likely to think that the outcome of a Scottish election matters. The evidence suggests that if voters do not see a parliament as being important they are less likely to turn out to vote.

However, a second possibility is that voters were already becoming disillusioned with the political process in 1997 (as the general election had a relatively low turnout compared with earlier elections) and by 1999 this disillusionment had become more widespread, leading voters to stay away from the polling booth. Table 4.4 looks at the extent to which disillusionment with politics had increased between the two elections. There are a number of ways in which disillusionment might be conceived and measured. The measure used here is a question that asked respondents whether or not they agreed that 'it doesn't much matter which party is in power, in the end things go on much the same'.

Table 4.4 Disillusionment with politics, 1997–1999

	It doesn't really matter who is in power	
	1997	*1999*
Agree strongly	8	8
Agree	35	48
Neither	19	9
Disagree	33	32
Disagree strongly	6	4
Sample size (=100%)	750	1,504

Source: Scottish Election Survey 1997, Scottish Parliamentary Election Survey 1999

The table shows a clear increase in the proportion agreeing that it doesn't much matter which party is in power: in 1997 the respondents were fairly evenly split but by 1999 over 50 per cent agreed. Furthermore, this increase in disillusionment is accompanied by a sharp decline in turnout among those who feel it doesn't matter who is in power. In 1997, 73 per cent of those who strongly agreed turned out to vote, compare with just 57 per cent in 1999. These figures suggest that we should not be too hasty in concluding that the lower turnout in 1999 was a characteristic of the Scottish Parliament; we will need to watch closely to see if this disillusionment causes a further fall in turnout in the next UK general election.

In addition to the relatively low turnout overall, Table 4.1 also pointed to a differential turnout among different groups of party supporters. In particular we found that turnout seemed to be especially low amongst those who had previously voted Labour. Further evidence to support this claim is found by looking at the preferred party of those who did not vote. Half of those who did not vote reported that, had they voted, their preferred party would have been Labour. It is tempting to put this down to deliberate abstention on the part of Labour supporters disaffected by the party's performance in government. Respondents who reported non-voting were asked their reason for this, enabling them to state that they had deliberately abstained from voting. However, there is no evidence to suggest that non-voters who state they would have voted Labour were more likely to say they deliberately abstained than those who preferred other parties. A range of other factors are stated by all non-voters, such as difficulties in getting to a polling station, work or sickness preventing them from voting, being away on election day and lack of interest. If it is not the case that Labour supporters were more likely to stay away from the polls deliberately, then we must find alternative explanations for the relatively low turnout among previous Labour voters.

One possible explanation may be that Labour supporters are drawn disproportionately from groups who are less likely to turn out to vote. In order to test, directly, whether or not these social factors explain the relatively low turnout figure among Labour supporters, a statistical model is used, which allows the effect of membership of different social groups to be taken into consideration while testing whether Labour supporters were less likely to vote. Table 4.5 shows the results of this model, a logistic regression model: the outcome variable is a two-category variable – did not vote versus voted. (For further details of this technique see Appendix.) In simple terms a positive value for a coefficient indicates an increased chance of turning out to vote, while a negative coefficient indicates an increased likelihood of being a non-voter. To test the proposition that previous Labour supporters were less likely to turn out to vote than supporters of other parties, variables indicating how the respondent voted in 1997 are included in the model. In addition to the first model which includes the socio-demographic variables to assess whether it is the basis of Labour's support which led to a lower turnout, a second model is also presented which includes two measures of attitudes and disillusionment – the relative importance of the Scottish Parliament compared with Westminster and the extent to which the respondent agreed that it doesn't matter who is in power.

The first model confirms the impact of socio-economic and demographic factors shown in Table 4.3. Educational level and housing tenure are the only economic variables to have a significant impact on turnout, while age is also a significant factor, with younger members of the electorate being less likely to turn out to vote. Of most interest in answering the question of differential turnout among party supporters are the coefficients associated with the respondent's vote in 1997. Each of the variables provides a contrast between that party's support and the Labour Party (in technical terms the Labour Party is our 'reference category' for this variable). Thus, a significant coefficient should be interpreted as the supporters of that party varying significantly from supporters of the Labour Party.

These coefficients show that those who voted SNP in 1997 were more likely to turn out to vote than those who voted Labour in 1997; this is not true of those who voted Conservative or Liberal Democrat. As already noted, those who didn't vote in 1997 were more likely than Labour supporters not to vote in 1999. This suggests that the SNP were more successful in getting their voters to turn out to vote in the Scottish Parliament elections than other parties and particularly the Labour Party.

The second model includes measures of the importance of the new parliament and a measure of whether or not it matters who is in power. We may have expected these measures to explain some of the difference between the turnout of Labour and SNP supporters, perhaps expecting that SNP supporters were more likely to consider

Table 4.5 Logistic regression model of turnout

	Model I		Model II	
	Coefficient	Standard Error	Coefficient	Standard error
Constant	1.042	not relevant	−0.072	not relevant
Social Class (Salariat)				
Routine non-manual	0.152	0.227	0.196	0.243
Petty bourgeoisie	−0.480	0.277	−0.491	0.294
Manual foreman	−0.394	0.300	−0.501	0.313
Working class	−0.097	0.217	−0.199	0.230
Education (degree):				
Higher education below				
degree level	−0.783★	0.277	−0.625★	0.285
A level/Highers	−0.904★	0.298	−0.700★	0.308
O level/CSE	−0.838★	0.280	−0.528	0.294
None	−0.924★	0.300	−0.460	0.317
Religion (Protestant):				
None	−0.287	0.165	−0.335	0.177
Roman Catholic	0.155	0.231	0.218	0.248
Other	−0.348	0.321	−0.428	0.332
Housing tenure (owners):				
Rents: Local authority	−0.128	0.184	0.000	0.200
Rents: Other	−0.833★	0.228	−0.907	0.237
Age in years	0.027★	0.005	0.027	0.006
Gender (male)	−0.253	0.153	−0.278	0.161
Vote in 1997 (Labour)				
Did not vote	−1.228★	0.187	−1.034★	0.200
Conservative	0.285	0.239	0.295	0.251
Liberal Democrat	−0.021	0.281	−0.004	0.296
SNP	0.858★	0.241	0.780★	0.248
Matters who is in power			0.276★	0.074
Scottish Parliament will				
have most influence			0.371★	0.151

In each case the reference category is shown brackets.
★ statistically significant at 5% level
Source: Scottish Parliamentary Election Survey 1999

the parliament important. However, the inclusion of these variables does not change the finding that those who had voted SNP in 1997 were more likely to turn out and vote in 1999 than those who had voted Labour.

This difference in turnout between supporters of Labour and the SNP is especially interesting. Earlier work in Scotland has highlighted the extent to which these two parties are competing for the same group of votes (Brand *et al.* 1994; Brown *et al.* 1999). Broadly speaking, both the SNP and Labour have traditionally drawn support from the lower end of the socio-economic scale, and from those with a strong sense of Scottish identity. Yet this evidence suggests that the SNP has been rather more successful in retaining its support at these elections. Some of the factors behind the Labour Party's performance were explored in Chapter 3, where the focus was on the difference between the vote achieved in the Scottish Parliament elections and the vote that would have been achieved in a Westminster election on the same day. The important question here is why SNP supporters were more likely to turn out to vote.

One possible explanation for this higher turnout may be the expectations and beliefs that groups of voters held about the Parliament. Perhaps SNP supporters had more interest in seeing the Parliament succeed? When asked if they would like to see the parliament abolished there are very small proportions of both sets of supporters who agree, with 8 per cent of Labour Party identifiers and 3 per cent of SNP identifiers wanting to see the Parliament abolished. However, we find a greater difference in beliefs about the powers the Parliament should have. Among SNP identifiers, 87 per cent would like to see the Parliament's powers increased while 57 per cent of Labour identifiers felt the same way.

In explaining the turnout of different groups of voters, we have so far focused on the characteristics of the electorate and of the institution they were electing, but it is equally likely that it is characteristics of the parties seeking to be elected that influenced whether or not people went to the polls. The Labour Party and the SNP have campaigned in Scotland in recent years as both working class and Scottish parties. Earlier work in Scotland has shown the extent to which class and nationality are linked together in the minds and belief systems of the Scottish people (Brand *et al.* 1994; Brown *et al.* 1999) and that to be seen as not supporting the working class often goes hand-in-hand with being seen as anti-Scottish. The extent to which these two parties have managed to retain their images as being for the working class and for Scotland may have strongly influenced the decisions of their former voters and will almost certainly affect their future electoral performances in Scotland. Table 4.6 shows the extent to which the parties were perceived as looking after the interests of working class people, middle-class people and Scots in general. For comparison the figures for Labour in 1997 are also included. Unfortunately the same question was not asked about the SNP in 1997 and so it is not possible to measure change in their party image.

Table 4.6 Perceptions of Labour looking after various interests, 1997–1999

	Perception of:			
	'New' Labour		Scottish Labour	SNP
	1997	1999	1999	1999
Looks after working-class interests:				
Very closely	35	5	9	13
Fairly closely	58	48	57	53
Not very closely	6	41	30	28
Not at all closely	2	6	4	6
Sample size (=100%)	731	1,118	1,115	1,103
Looks after middle-class interests:				
Very closely	12	10	7	8
Fairly closely	76	65	64	57
Not very closely	11	23	26	28
Not at all closely	1	2	3	8
Sample size (=100%)	715	1,096	1,089	1,080
Looks after Scottish interests:				
Very closely	not asked	2	7	24
Fairly	not asked	40	56	48
Not very closely	not asked	46	29	21
Not at all closely	not asked	12	7	7
Sample size (=100%)		1,100	1,093	1,099

Scource: Scottish Parliamentary Election Survey 1999, Scottish Election Survey 1997

The fall in the image of Labour as a party that looks after working-class interests is dramatic. In 1997, 93 per cent of the Scottish electorate believed that the Labour Party looked after working-class interests either very or fairly closely; just two years later that had slipped to 53 per cent. Although the image of Scottish Labour is slightly better, with 66 per cent saying they look after working-class interests either very or fairly closely, this is still well below the level immediately after the election of the Labour government at West-minster. Scottish Labour may take some comfort from the fact that the electorate sees the SNP as only being as good as they are at looking after working-class interests, 66 per cent believing the SNP look after working-class interests either very or fairly closely. However, it remains to be seen how well Scottish Labour can assert an independent image in Scotland or whether the electoral fortunes of Labour in Scotland will be driven by images of what the Labour government in Westminster is doing and saying.

When considering how well the parties look after middle-class interests, the Labour party and Scottish Labour both fare better than the SNP, with three out of four people believing that New Labour looks after middle-class interests very or fairly closely. In fact in 1999 New Labour is perceived as a party that looks after middle-class interests more than one which looks after the working class.

Finally we can look at perceptions of the parties as looking after Scots in general. Here there is some indication that there may be a cause for concern for the Labour Party. Only two out of five believe that New Labour looks after Scots interests very or fairly closely, compared with almost three out of four who believe that the SNP do. Again we find that Scottish Labour is perceived more favourably than New Labour, but still less favourably than the SNP. These party images are of particular importance in Scotland, where (as we shall see in Chapters 8 and 9) the electorate favour a broadly left-wing political agenda and where working-class and national identities have played a prominent role in political debates. They also indicate the main sources of divide in Scottish electoral politics, and it is the competition for votes between Labour and the SNP to which we now turn.

PARTY COMPETITION

In the previous section we saw how the image of the Labour Party has changed in the short period since they gained power at Westminster. The extent to which this change in image will impact on their electoral support is in some measure dependent on the perceptions and policies of the SNP, and on the extent to which the parties continue to compete for the votes of the same segments of the electorate. In this section we consider the possibilities for future party competition by looking at the current similarities and differences between Labour and SNP supporters. In addition to the next election to the Scottish Parliament, this is also of crucial importance in the next UK general election. Whereas in England disaffected Labour supporters have few choices, in Scotland the SNP may be a real alternative to those with broadly left-of-centre attitudes (a point to which we return in Chapter 8).

The first question, therefore, is the extent to which Labour and SNP supporters share a common belief or value system. Here we make use of attitudinal scales developed to understand the belief systems underpinning the British electorate. The first two scales developed by Heath *et al.*(1994) measure the two traditional dimensions of political attitudes – a left-right (socialist–*laissez-faire*) scale and a liberal–authoritarian scale. In addition to these scales, two further scales are used, measuring British nationalism and Scottish nationalism respectively (Heath *et al.* 1999). Each scale consists of an aggregation of individual survey items designed to measure different aspects of the underlying belief system. The socialist–*laissez-faire*, liberal-authoritarian and British nationalism scales each consist of six survey items and can therefore take values ranging from 6 to 30 (each item has responses 1–5 ranging from 'agree strongly' to 'disagree strongly').The Scottish nationalism scale attempts to mirror the British scale but has only five items and can, therefore, take values from 5 to 25. Low values on the scales represent the socialist, liberal and nationalist positions respectively. For further details of the items used in creating these scales, see the Appendix.

Table 4.7 shows the mean position on each of the scales for each group of party supporters (the measure used here is the party the respondents identify most closely with). This table gives a picture of the value positions of different groups of supporters and therefore the distances between the supporters of different parties. If the supporters of different parties have very different value systems we would expect there to be little exchange of support between them; however, if the supporters of different parties hold similar underlying value systems we would expect there to be greater fluidity of support between them.

The scales seem to separate the parties in two key directions. On the socialist–*laissez-faire* scale and the liberal–authoritarian scale supporters of the Conservative party clearly stand out from supporters of other parties, being more 'right-wing' on both scales – that is, more *laissez-faire* and more authoritarian. However, on these two scales Labour and SNP supporters cannot be distinguished. Supporters of both parties hold values that are more socialist and more liberal than the Conservatives. This suggests that on policies relating to economic inequalities and tolerance, the supporters of both the SNP and Labour would share common objectives.

Table 4.7 Position on value scales by party identity

	Party identity				
	None	*Conservative*	*Labour*	*Liberal Democrat*	*SNP*
Value scales					
Socialist–*laissez-faire*	15.93	18.16	14.74	16.29	14.79
	(Cons)	(All)	(Cons/Lib)	(Cons/Lab/SNP)	(Cons/Lib)
Liberal–authoritarian	18.43	19.72	18.39	17.94	17.92
	(Lab/Lib/SNP)	(Cons)	(Cons)	(Cons)
British nationalism	17.45	16.32	17.37	17.82	18.97
	(SNP)	(Lab/Lib/SNP)	(Cons/SNP)	(Cons/SNP)	(All)
Scottish nationalism	14.78	15.32	14.67	15.10	12.86
	(SNP)	(Lab/SNP)	(Cons/SNP)	(SNP)	(All)

For meaning of scales, see Appendix.
Figures in brackets indicate which other party supporters differ significantly.
Source: Scottish Parliamentary Election Survey 1999

The nationalism scales show a rather different picture; again we find that the Conservative supporters stand out from everyone else, being more British nationalist and less Scottish nationalist than supporters of other parties. However, we also find a significant difference between Labour party supporters and SNP supporters. While both groups are less British nationalist and more Scottish nationalist than the Conservative supporters, SNP supporters are also more Scottish nationalist and less British nationalist than Labour supporters. This is in line with earlier work that has suggested that the key difference between the supporters of Labour and the SNP was their attitudes towards the constitution (Brand *et al.* 1994).

In conjunction with the changes in the image of the Labour Party discussed above, these findings suggest that the party must take care not to alienate its supporters further as there is a real alternative for disenchanted supporters in the SNP in terms of ideological position.

Table 4.8 Logistic regression model of SNP vs. Labour voting, 1997–1999

	1997		1999	
	Coefficient	Standard Error	Coefficient	Standard error
Constant	−6.920	not relevant	1.792	not relevant
Value Scales				
Socialist–*laissez-faire*	0.154★	0.042	0.056	0.037
Liberal–authoritarian	0.020	0.045	−0.014	0.042
British nationalism	0.316★	0.050	0.186★	0.045
Scottish nationalism	−0.212★	0.048	−0.322★	0.050
Social Class (Salariat):				
Routine non-manual	−0.970	0.411	−0.284	0.364
Petty bourgeoisie	0.920★	0.461	0.398	0.469
Manual foremen	−0.464	0.493	−0.405	0.459
Working class	0.098	0.356	−0.318	0.337
Education (degree):				
Higher education below degree level	0.545	0.476	0.021	0.405
A level/Highers	0.786	0.533	−0.096	0.471
O level/CSE	0.146	0.508	0.160	0.423
None	1.040★	0.526	0.764	0.455
Religion (Protestants):				
None	−0.373	0.281	−0.337	0.259
Roman Catholic	−1.534★	0.443	−1.115★	0.349
Other	−0.205	0.534	−0.003	0.555
Housing tenure (owners):				
Rents: Local authority	0.339	0.299	−0.329	0.289
Rents: Other	−0.545	0.540	−0.353	0.508
Age in years	−0.008	0.009	−0.022★	0.009
Gender (male)	−0.444	0.265	−0.232	0.240
National identity (Equally Scottish and British)				
Scottish not British	0.411	0.403	0.072	0.337
Scottish more than British	0.830★	0.378	−0.085	0.312
British more than Scottish	−0.714	1.421	−0.739	0.907
British not Scottish	−5.091	9.232	−2.510	1.372

In each case the reference category is shown in brackets.
★ statistically significant at 5% level
Source: Scottish Parliamentary Election Survey 1999

However, the traditional attachment to the Labour Party of particular social groups within Scotland may help them retain their support. Table 4.8 presents the findings of logistic regression models designed to test the differences in support for Labour and the SNP. In each model only those who voted either for the Labour Party or the SNP are included; thus where coefficients are statistically significant they indicate a factor that is relevant in distinguishing between these two groups of voters. Two models are presented. The second looks at the differences between Labour and SNP supporters in the constituency vote at the Scottish Parliament election; the first looks at the vote at the 1997 general election. In each model it is SNP voting that is the dependent variable, and so a positive coefficient indicates an increased likelihood to vote SNP over Labour while a negative coefficient indicates an increased likelihood to vote Labour over SNP.

There are few differences across the two models, indicating that there has been little change in the factors distinguishing Labour and SNP support between 1997 and 1999 (though we should remember this includes only the constituency ballot). One factor which does change over time is the position of the respondent on the socialist–*laissez-faire* scale; this was a significant distinguishing factor at the 1997 general election (with those taking a more left-wing position being more likely to vote Labour). However, by 1999 this was no longer a distinguishing factor between the two groups of supporters, again giving a warning to Labour that on issues that lie broadly on a 'left–right' dimension it has a serious risk of losing support to the SNP. (This point is analysed further in Chapter 8.) In all of the models presented, the key factors distinguishing the two groups are positions on the two nationalism scales, those with higher scores on the British nationalism scale (that is, a less British nationalist outlook) being more likely to vote SNP and those with high scores on the Scottish nationalism scale (in other words, a weaker nationalist position) being more likely to vote Labour. In addition we find that across all models religion plays an important part in distinguishing between Labour and SNP support, Roman Catholics being less likely to vote for the SNP. This relationship between Labour support and the Roman Catholic population in Scotland has been a persistent feature of electoral politics over the last thirty years, but it is interesting to note that it has been maintained into the first elections to the Scottish Parliament.

The findings of these models add further weight to the possibility that Labour could lose support to the SNP, particularly among groups with a strong sense of Scottish national identity. Although there remains a tie between Labour support and religion, there are no other such differences among social groups that could underpin Labour support. As Labour seem no longer to be able to rely on an ideological difference on a left-right dimension, there are clear dangers for the party in the weakening perceptions that they work in the interests of Scotland. When asked if they trusted Labour to work in Scotland's interests, it is only among Labour party identifiers that there is a majority in 1999 who trust it to do so 'just about always' or 'most of the time'. Among all other groups within the electorate a majority trust Labour to work in Scotland's interests at best 'some of the time'. This is a sharp contrast to the position at the time of the 1997 general election when practically a majority of all groups trusted Labour at least 'most of the time' (Brown et al. 1999). These figures may provide a strong warning to the Labour government that, while its record in office will have some influence on the Scottish electorate, they must convince the Scottish people that they are act-ing in Scotland's best interests. In the general elections of 1992 and 1997 the Conservative party paid heavily for the perception that they were an anti-Scottish party (Brown et al. 1999) and, while currently trust in the Labour Party has not reached the low levels experienced by the Conservatives in 1997, it has fallen very rapidly in a short time-span. As Chapter 3 has shown, elections to the Scottish Parliament may hinge on the answers the parties give to Scottish questions; it is also possible that the answers given to those questions will influence future elections to the Westminster parliament.

CONCLUSION

This chapter has considered changes in the support for the parties in Scotland since the 1997 general election. It has focused in particular on the fortunes of the Labour Party, showing that Labour failed to hold on to a large part of the support it gained in 1997. The reasons behind this decline are complex; in part it is a result of previous Labour voters not turning out to vote for the party in 1999, but it is also due to some haemorrhaging of support from Labour to the SNP. Our analysis suggests that the image of the Labour Party in Scotland has suffered since their election to government at Westminster, with a clear message that it is no longer seen as looking after Scotland and the working class. These images are all the more important when Labour finds itself in a position of competition with a party – the SNP – that has a similar ideological position and social basis of support.

NOTE

1. As this relies on a recall of an earlier election it is likely to contain some misreporting. There is likely to be a tendency to over-report turning out to vote and also to recall voting for the same party as in the 1999 elections. However, there is no reason to suppose that this tendency will be greater among different groups of voters. In addition, the tables using this measure were checked against a panel study of the electorate and show the same overall trends (see Appendix). The panel study data were not used for this analysis because of high levels of attrition among non-voters.

5

NEW SYSTEM, NEW VOTERS?

―᾿ᴀᴘᴘᴘᴏᴀᴀᴀᴀᴠ―

INTRODUCTION

The election to the Scottish Parliament was historic not only in being the first election to a Scottish legislature in 300 years; it was also the first national election in Britain to be held fully under a system of proportional representation (PR). The impact of the system in terms of the results of the election is clear. The SNP gained seats in proportion to their total vote allowing them to form the opposition to Labour in the Parliament to match the opposition they had been at elections over the previous two decades. The Conservative Party in Scotland, left in disarray after their performance in the general election two years earlier, was able to regain some parliamentary representation in Scotland. The system also gave representation to smaller parties such as the Scottish Socialists and the Greens (for more detailed analysis see Chapter 2). However, it is not this impact at the aggregate level that is the concern of this chapter. The chapter focuses on the relationship between the electoral system and the electorate. First we consider how the electorate received the new system; the extent to which the system is understood by and transparent to the electorate may affect trust in the Parliament and the way in which it is received. Second, we consider the way in which the electoral system influenced the behaviour of the electorate. Did the introduction of PR change the way in which the Scottish electorate voted, or did voters continue to vote as they had always done but with the system converting those votes into a rather different outcome?

The electoral system adopted for the election is a variant of proportional representation known as the Additional Member System. Under this system voters cast two votes, one for a constituency member and a second for a party list. The constituency members, of whom there are seventy-three in the Scottish Parliament, are elected using the familiar first-past-the-post system. The members taken from the party lists are then used as a 'top-up' to ensure that the total distribution of seats in the Parliament reflects, as closely as possible, the distribution of votes on the second ballot. For the purposes of this second ballot Scotland was divided into eight separate regions, with seven members elected from each regional list, and so we refer to this ballot as the regional element.[1] The effects of this 'top-up' system are best illustrated by example. In the constituency vote Labour gained fifty-three (73 per cent) of constituency seats with 39 per cent of the constituency votes. The SNP on the other hand gained just seven (10 per cent) of constituency seats from 29 per cent of the constituency votes. The 'top-up' seats aim to rectify this disproportionality; however, with over half of the seats allocated by a first-past-the-post system, the regional vote cannot fully compensate for disproportionality on the constituency vote. Thus the Labour party is allocated only three seats from the regional lists while the SNP have twenty-eight seats from lists, correcting some but not all of the over-representation of Labour who retain 43 per cent of the seats with just 34 per cent of the regional vote.

It is the effect of the introduction of this system on the behaviour of the electorate that is considered in this chapter. The results from the constituency ballot suggest that much of the political map of Scotland remained unchanged, only three of the seventy-three constituencies returning a member from a different party from the one they had elected in the 1997 general election (Falkirk West, Inverness East and Lochaber, and Aberdeen South). Chapter 4 examined the factors behind this voting decision and compared it with the 1997 general election, concluding that overall a large proportion of the Scottish electorate voted in the same way on this constituency vote as they had done in 1997. However, the ballot for the regional lists has no such precedent and while its overall distribution broadly reflected that of the constituency vote at the aggregate level (with some crucial differences discussed below) further exploration is required of the factors influencing voting decisions at the individual level. The key question addressed in this chapter is, then, the extent to which a new electoral system in Scotland produced a new kind of voter.

UNDERSTANDING AND ACCEPTANCE OF THE SYSTEM

The debate about electoral reform in the United Kingdom has seen opponents of PR identify four main features of the systems that they believe make them inappropriate for use in UK general elections (Jenkins 1998). Systems of PR are seen to be more complicated than the familiar first-past-the-post system, and certainly the system adopted for the Scottish Parliament election was more difficult to understand than the system used for UK general elections. However, whether or not more complicated means also too complicated remains an issue for debate. Farrell and Gallagher (1999) draw a distinction between understanding the system at different levels, for example understanding the ballot papers and voting decisions sufficiently to use the system (that is, to cast votes), and understanding the mechanics of the system in enough detail to make informed and possibly tactical decisions as to how to cast votes.

Before the election to the Scottish Parliament took place, the government carried out an extensive voter education campaign, designed to encourage people to vote and to ensure that the new system was widely understood (see Chapter 2). Figures from the Scottish Parliament Election Survey show that the campaign reached a wide audience, with 83 per cent of respondents saying they had seen the adverts and 77 per cent indicating that they had read or seen the leaflet. However, the effectiveness of an education campaign cannot be measured in terms of simply reaching its target audience; it must also be assessed by the level of knowledge of that audience.

Table 5.1 shows how difficult the voters found two aspects of the new system, namely the completion of the ballot paper and the ways in which votes were converted into seats. These two aspects represent two different elements of the system; the first is essential for voters to be able to cast their votes under the new system, while the second is not necessary in order to vote but is an important part of understanding what it is the system does. These aspects broadly represent the levels of understanding identified by Farrell and Gallagher. There are clear differences shown between how difficult voters found the ballot papers and how difficult they found the actual system of allocating seats. Only 10 per cent found ballot papers to be 'very' or 'fairly' difficult to complete while almost 50 per cent found the allocation of seats 'very' or 'fairly' difficult to understand. In addition, when these two questions were broken down between those who had and had not seen the advertisements and leaflets in the government's education campaign no significant differences were found, suggesting that although the campaign reached a wide audience its impact was limited. (For a detailed evaluation of the voter education campaign see Scotland Office (2000).) This divide in the perception of difficulty (between the act of casting a vote and how the votes cast are translated into seats) has a direct bearing on debates about the understanding of systems of PR; it is possible to argue that voters do not need to fully understand the mechanics of the electoral system in order to vote. To cast a vote all that is required is an understanding of the ballot papers, which the vast majority of respondents have. However, if voters are to make more sophisticated and tactical decisions about how to cast their votes then a greater understanding of the electoral system is needed. It is, for example, a possibly greater understanding of the first-past-the-post system that has led to an increase in tactical voting at recent general elections.

Table 5.1 Experience of new voting system

	How difficult	
	Filling in ballot papers	Understanding how seats are worked out
Very difficult	1	9
Fairly difficult	9	39
Not very difficult	41	39
Not at all	49	14
Sample size (=100%)	1,007	991

Excludes those who did not answer.
Source: Scottish Parliamentary Election Survey 1999

Table 5.2 looks at the impact of these levels of understanding on behaviour, in terms of turning out to vote. Did a lack of understanding of the system cause voters to stay away from the polls?

There is some evidence to suggest that non-voting and understanding of the system are related. Of those who claimed to find understanding the ballot papers 'not at all difficult' just 8 per cent did not turn out to vote while among other groups around 20 per cent did not vote.[2] By contrast, there is no relationship between turnout and understanding of how the system converts votes into seats. This suggests that voters may be put off voting when faced with the prospect of a ballot paper that they find difficult to understand, in other words if voters do not feel confident about *using* the system. However, it would appear from these data that an understanding of exactly how the system produces a final outcome is not necessary for the public to turn out and vote.

Table 5.2 Non-voting by experience of new voting system

	Did not vote (%)	Sample size (=100%)
Ballot papers		
Very difficult	50	18
Fairly difficult	22	100
Not very difficult	20	406
Not at all	8	483
Votes to seats		
Very difficult	25	93
Fairly difficult	17	377
Not very difficult	19	385
Not at all	15	136

Excludes those who did not answer.
Source: Scottish Parliamentary Election Survey 1999

The questions shown in Tables 5.1 and 5.2 provide a subjective interpretation of voter understanding; that is, they ask how well voters *believe* they understood the system. This element is important, as it is their own perceptions of how well they understand the system that are likely to influence how voters respond to it. As Table 5.2 shows, those who felt they did not understand the ballot papers were much less likely to vote. However, it is also important to look at understanding of the system in a more objective way. Table 5.3 looks at a range of questions about the workings of the electoral system to test levels of voter knowledge about factual statements about the system. Each respondent was asked to say whether six statements about the electoral system were true or false. The respondents had the following options: definitely true, probably true, probably not true, definitely not true and can't choose. As the system was a new experience for the voters, the responses 'can't choose' and 'don't know' are left in for the purposes of the analysis as these may indicate confusion about the system. The six statements are listed below:

1: 'You are allowed to vote for the same party on the first and second vote.'

2: 'People are given two votes so they can show their first and second preference.'

3: 'The number of seats won by each party is decided by the number of first votes they get.'

4: 'Unless a party wins at least 5 per cent of the second vote it is unlikely to win any regional party list seats.'

5: 'Regional party list seats are allocated to try to make sure each party has as fair a share of the seats as possible.'

6: 'No candidate who stands in a constituency contest can be elected as a regional party list member.'

For each statement the proportion answering correctly is the combined proportion in the 'definitely' and 'probably' categories. For example, for number 1, which is in fact true, the proportion correct are all those who answered either definitely true or probably true.

Some aspects of the system appear to be better understood by voters than others. The first statement (on voting for the same party twice) has by far the most 'correct' responses, with 78 per cent answering correctly. As this question relates to actual behaviour of voters we might expect to find high levels of knowledge; after all, many of those surveyed had already turned out and voted for the same party twice. At the other end of the scale only 26 per cent correctly responded to the statement on first and second preferences, showing some confusion about exactly what was being decided by the two ballots (we come back to this possible confusion below). There are also high levels of non-response to some of these statements. Over 40 per cent of respondents could not choose an answer

71

to number 6 (whether a constituency candidate could subsequently be elected from a regional party list), suggesting that some aspects of the system, in particular the mechanics and regulations, remained a mystery to large proportions of the electorate.

Table 5.3 Knowledge of new voting system

	Correct answer	% Correct	% Can't choose
Vote for same party on first and second vote	True	78	17
Two votes to express first and second preference	False	26	16
No. of seats won decided by no. of first votes	False	30	24
If not win 5% of list vote get no seats	True	43	38
Regional list seats to give fair share	True	63	26
Constituency candidate can't be elected from list	False	31	42

Sample size in each row: 1165
Source: Scottish Parliamentary Election Survey 1999

The data in Table 5.3 also highlight the divide shown in Table 5.1. Generally speaking there are good levels of understanding of the basics of the electoral system, which parties can be voted for and roughly what the system is designed to do, as shown in statements 1 and 5. Questions that ask in more detail about the electoral system show lower levels of knowledge, for example 2 and 6. We might expect that this will rise over time as the electorate become more accustomed to the system and to the media statistics explaining the way the system works. Evidence from New Zealand supports this: see the New Zealand Election Study on the Web at www.nzes.org.

The remaining criticisms of PR focus on particular aspects of the systems. It is argued that systems of PR often (in fact usually) produce coalition governments, that they entail some kind of multi-member constituencies and that (in the case of the system adopted for the Scottish election) operate a closed list system whereby it is the political parties and not the voters directly who choose the members elected from the regional party lists. It is argued that these features are unpopular with the British public and are, therefore, reasons why PR should not be adopted for elections in Britain (and furthermore are reasons why any campaign and referendum vote on the introduction of PR for Westminster would fail). The remainder of this section looks in detail at these claims and the extent to which these views are found among the Scottish electorate.

We begin by considering overall levels of support for the electoral system adopted for the Scottish Parliament election. Respondents were asked two questions relating to their support of the new electoral system. The first was:

> Some people prefer the new way of voting for the Scottish Parliament as they say it means all parties are fairly represented. Others say that the old way of voting used in elections to the UK House of Commons is better as it produces effective government. Which view comes closer to your own?

The second question asked:

> How much do you agree or disagree that the Scottish parliament should be elected using proportional representation?

The degree of similarity of the responses to these questions is remarkable. On the first question, 66 per cent of respondents were in favour of keeping the system of PR, while on the second question 67 per cent of respondents either strongly agreed or agreed that the elections should be held using PR. As we shall see below it is usual in Britain to find a high degree of variability in responses to questions about electoral reform for the Westminster elections, depending on how the question is asked (Curtice and Jowell 1997). The very fact that no such variation is found here suggests that attitudes towards PR for elections to the Scottish Parliament are much more firmly set in people's minds. Thus, on the face of it at least, we find that the Scottish people seem to be in favour of the electoral system adopted. But to what extent do the criticisms discussed above find a resonance among the Scottish electorate: is there any evidence to suggest that those who find these arguments convincing are less likely to be in favour of the system?

Turning first to the criticism of PR systems that they frequently produce coalition governments that are unpopular with the British public, evidence from the British Social Attitudes series has often shown the public to be evenly split between those for and against

73

coalition rule (Curtice and Jowell 1997). At the time our fieldwork was conducted, it was clear that a coalition government would be formed in Scotland between Labour and the Liberal Democrats although it was too early in the life of the Parliament for the performance of that coalition to have influenced attitudes towards multi-party rule. On each of the measures of attitudes to coalition government included in the survey, a small majority of respondents favoured coalition rule over government by a single party. This was true of preferences not only for government in the Scottish Parliament but also for government at Westminster: 56 per cent of respondents favoured coalition government in Edinburgh with 52 per cent favouring it for Westminster. However, respondents seemed to be slightly less in favour of the idea of secret pacts and coalition deals: when asked if parties should make public possible coalition partners before the elections, 61 per cent either strongly agreed or agreed that they should. While the Scottish public are by no means opposed to coalition rule, they would prefer to have some idea of how those possible coalitions might be formed.

The argument of opponents of PR that – because systems of PR are more likely to produce coalition governments which are unpopular with voters PR itself would also be unpopular – does not appear to be supported by our findings. Although those who favoured coalitions were slightly more supportive of the electoral system, among both those who do and do not favour coalition rule in Edinburgh there was a majority of support for PR in elections to the Scottish parliament, with 61 per cent of those who favoured single-party government and 74 per cent of those who favoured a coalition either strongly agreeing or agreeing that the Scottish Parliament should be elected using a system of PR.

The third objection raised by opponents of PR is that it entails multi-member constituencies, with the result that lines of accountability and representation are unclear. Earlier survey evidence in Britain has suggested that voters have a strong attachment to single-member constituencies (Dunleavy et al. 1997). Farrell and Gallagher (1999) suggest that this attachment may be due to a misunderstanding on the part of voters about the role of MPs in multi-member constituencies.

Among the Scottish public, 73 per cent would rather have a single MP than a multi-member constituency, lending some support to the objection of opponents to PR. However, as with those opposed to coalitions, we find that there remains a majority in favour of the electoral system among those who prefer to have a single MP to represent their views. Of the latter, 65 per cent either strongly agreed or agreed that the Scottish Parliament should be elected by PR, compared with 77 per cent amongst those who preferred to have more than one constituency MP.

The final objection raised by opponents of the system introduced for the Scottish Parliament elections is that it used a closed list system for the members elected from the party lists. Closed lists allow voters to express a preference for a party but not to distinguish between individual candidates put forward by that party. Under this system the members elected are decided by their order on the party list, which in turn is determined by the political parties. To understand the views of the Scottish electorate, two questions were asked about the issue of closed party lists:

> I would prefer to have been able to vote for individual candidates on the regional list vote rather than for a party list.

> Parties, not voters, should decide which of the candidates on their regional list get the seats the party has won.

In each case respondents were asked whether they agreed with the statement on a 5-point scale from strongly agree to strongly disagree. In each case there is clear support for the idea that it should not be parties who decide who is elected from the list. The first question has 49 per cent agreeing that they would have preferred to vote for individual candidates, while on the second question 52 per cent disagreed that it should be parties who choose. Again there seems to be some evidence to support the claims made by opponents of PR that closed lists are unpopular with voters. However, as with earlier questions, despite disliking this aspect of the system, voters remain in favour of the system as a whole. Among those who said that they would have preferred to vote for individuals rather than a closed list, 67 per cent are in favour of the system of PR for elections to the Scottish Parliament, and amongst those who disagreed with party control of the lists, 70 per cent were in favour of the system of PR.

A very clear pattern emerges from looking at these criticisms of PR. In each case there is some evidence that the Scottish public recognises the weaknesses of the system, and that it is often split as to the desirability of specific features of the system.Yet despite this there remains clear support for the use of PR to elect the Scottish Parliament, even among those who are opposed to specific features. Further analysis gives some clues as to the reasons why this support for the system is found. Table 5.4 looks at responses to a series of statements about the electoral system, both positive and negative.

Table 5.4 Views on effects of new voting system

	New system leads to unstable government	New system too much power to small parties	New system much fairer	More point voting
Strongly agree	4	3	13	11
Agree	13	16	49	60
Neither	33	32	27	22
Disagree	43	44	10	6
Strongly disagree	7	6	2	–
Sample size (=100%)	985	1025	1004	1011

Source: Scottish Parliamentary Election Survey 1999

Table 5.4 demonstrates clearly that the Scottish public does not see the undesirable consequences of PR that opponents stress as problems. When asked if the new system would lead to unstable government and if the new system gave too much power to small parties, fewer than one in five agreed, with half disagreeing. On the positive side, 71 per cent thought that the new system meant that there was more point in voting, and 62 per cent believed the new system was 'much fairer than the one usually used at elections'.

Support for the system is an important part of the legitimation of the Parliament; it is essential to the effectiveness of a democratic institution that there is support for the way in which it was elected. The battle over PR for elections to the Scottish Parliament appears to be won, with majority support for the electoral system and little criticism of the over-arching principle of PR, albeit with some concern over specific parts of the system such as closed lists.

However, less clear-cut is the position on electoral reform for the House of Commons. Again, respondents were asked two questions:

> Some people say we should change the voting system for general elections to the UK House of Commons to allow smaller

political parties to get a fairer share of MPs. Others say that we should keep the voting system for the House of Commons as it is to produce effective government. Which view comes closer to your own?

and

How much do you agree or disagree that the UK should introduce proportional representation so that the number of MPs each party gets in the House of Commons matches more closely the number of votes each party gets?

Here we find a considerable difference in opinion dependent on the wording of the question. On the first of these questions, only 43 per cent were in favour of changing the voting system for the House of Commons, while on the second question 62 per cent either agreed or strongly agreed that the House of Commons should be elected using PR. These responses suggest that, while there is not widespread opposition to the idea of PR, there is variability according to exactly what respondents are asked and which elements of the outcomes of PR are emphasised. This sensitivity may suggest that, as yet, attitudes to PR for Westminster elections have not become strongly formulated in the minds of the electorate; they are swayed in different directions when presented with the different positive and negative aspects of changing the system. This is likely to mean that any referendum campaign could hinge on which aspects of the effects of change are most convincingly put across to the electorate. It appears possible to persuade the electorate of both the need for proportionality for fairness and also the need to preserve 'strong government'. The extent to which one side is able to make a more convincing argument could well sway what is likely to be a close referendum decision.

VOTING BEHAVIOUR AND THE ELECTORAL SYSTEM

The remainder of this chapter focuses on the way in which the elec-torate voted under the new electoral system. Chapter 3 considered the change and continuity between votes cast at a hypothetical UK general election and the constituency vote at the Scottish Parliament election, and Chapter 4 examined change and continuity between the 1997 general election and the Scottish Parliament election. In this section the relationship between the vote on the constituency ballot and the vote for the regional list is considered. To what extent did the electorate vote differently under the new system? Did the electorate respond to the new tactical situations in different ways or did voters merely continue to vote in the same way they had always done?

Table 5.5 shows the relationship between the two votes cast. (Non-voters are excluded from analysis in the chapter; for a detailed analysis of non-voting see Chapter 4.) Overall, around one in five of those who voted at the elections cast their votes differently (known as ticket-splitting), a small but not insignificant proportion. Of all the main parties, the Conservatives retained the highest proportion of the constituency ballot in the regional list vote, with 89 per cent of those who voted Conservative on the first vote also voting Conservative on the second. This is perhaps to be expected. As we saw in Chapter 4, Conservative voters are likely to be quite distinct from those of the other parties in terms of ideological positions, and so there are few natural choices other than Conservative for those of a generally right-of-centre position. Among the other parties, there is no clear pattern of support switching between one party and another. However, again reflecting the ideological divide, fewer of the supporters of other parties in the constituency vote switch to Conservative in the regional vote than to any other single party.

Table 5.5 Relationship between regional vote and constituency vote

Regional Vote	Constituency vote				
	Conservative	Labour	Lib. Dem.	SNP	Other
Conservative	89	3	3	1	–
Labour	1	79	8	6	24
Liberal Democrat	4	6	77	4	12
SNP	3	7	3	83	35
Other	2	5	8	6	29
Sample size (=100%)	145	428	139	287	17

Excludes non-voters.
Source: Scottish Parliamentary Election Survey 1999

One of the arguments of the pro-PR campaigners is that, in a system of PR, voters can cast their votes more sincerely as there is less

chance of 'wasted' votes. However, the system adopted for the
Scottish Parliament election retains some of the features of the first-
past-the-post system (especially in the constituency ballot) so that in
some circumstances there is every chance of votes being 'wasted' and
the tactical situation being important. If this argument is correct we
would expect to find lower levels of reported tactical voting in these
elections than was the case in 1997, an election which was itself
characterised by high levels of anti-Conservative tactical voting
(Curtice and Steed 1997). One way of assessing levels of tactical
voting is to look at the reasons voters give for casting their votes in
particular ways. Table 5.6 looks at the reasons given by voters for
their vote in the 1997 general election and the two votes in the 1999
Scottish Parliament election.

Table 5.6 Reasons for party choice, 1997–1999

	1997	1999 Constituency	1999 Region
Always vote that way	31	34	31
Best party	51	50	57
Really preferred another party but no chance	10	6	4
Candidate not party	2	4	1
Other tactical	2	2	3
Other	4	3	5
Sample size (=100%)	700	1,026	1,024

Sources: Scottish Election Survey 1997, Scottish Parliamentary Election Survey 1999

On the constituency ballot, there are three main reasons for a possible
tactical vote (that is a vote which does not express the first-choice
party of the voter). These are that the preferred party did not have
a chance of winning in that constituency (this would include the
possibility that the first-choice party was not standing in that constituency), to prevent an unpopular party from winning, or as a personal vote for a particular candidate rather than for the party they
represent. Table 5.6 suggests that overall levels of tactical voting on
the constituency vote in 1999 were similar to those of 1997, perhaps
unsurprisingly since this ballot took place over the same constituencies
(with the exception of Orkney and Shetland) and with the same
electoral system. In contrast the regional vote shows slightly lower
levels of tactical voting, with just 8 per cent of voters giving reasons

that could be interpreted as tactical compared with 14 per cent and 12 per cent respectively in 1997 and on the constituency vote in 1999.

However, with two ballots and the new electoral system the possibilities for new forms of tactical voting were increased, and the options offered to voters by the parties differed: for example, the Scottish Green Party did not stand in the constituency ballots at all. It was widely known that the first-past-the-post system would favour Labour, and so – in most parts of the country – a vote for Labour on the regional vote may have been perceived as 'wasted' as they were unlikely to gain many top-up seats from the lists. It is also possible that voters used the two votes to express their coalition preferences, as it was already seen as likely that no one party would achieve an overall majority. Using the survey data it is possible to disentangle some of the different types of tactical voting and ticket-splitting that were prevalent in the behaviour of the electorate.

Table 5.7 **Reasons for party choice, by whether voted same way in constituency and region**

Reasons for voting	Voted same way twice		Switched parties	
	Constituency	Region	Constituency	Region
Always vote that way	38	37	17	8
Best party	51	54	46	66
Really preferred another party but no chance	3	3	16	4
Candidate not party	2	1	12	2
Other tactical	2	2	2	6
Other	4	3	7	13
Sample size (=100%)	820	821	194	195

Sources: Scottish Parliamentary Election Survey 1999

Table 5.7 looks at the different reasons for the votes given by those who did and did not split their votes across two parties. In line with the way in which they voted, those who voted for the same party twice gave a broadly similar set of answers to both questions, with over one-third answering that they always vote that way. Relatively few of this group of voters gave any kind of tactical reasons for their choices: 7 per cent gave tactical reasons for their constituency vote and 6 per cent for their regional vote. Amongst those who changed their vote between the two ballot papers there are some marked differences. The proportion of this group answering that they always vote that way is much smaller, just 17 per cent on the constituency vote and 8 per cent on the regional vote. Furthermore on the regional vote two in three stated that they had voted for the best party, an indication that there may well have been more 'sincere' voting among this group on the vote that was conducted purely on PR.

There are also clear indications that the ticket-splitters were considerably more likely to be tactical voters of one kind or other. On the constituency ballot, 16 per cent of ticket-splitters said that they had really preferred another party who had no chance of winning, while a further 12 per cent said that they had voted for a candidate rather than the party. In total, 30 per cent of ticket-splitters gave reasons for their first vote that could be considered as tactical. This contrasts with just 12 per cent saying they had voted tactically on the regional ballot.

The survey data are not able to assess many of the subtleties of voting decisions under the Additional Member System. While the survey is able to give a good general indication of the levels of support for parties and policies, it is unable to analyse the distinctive political situation in each of the constituency and regional settings. The data in the tables give us an indication of the ways in which decisions were made; we can see that where voters did cast their votes for different parties this was often reported as being dependent on either a local candidate or the local tactical situation. What we are able to conclude is that there is a sizeable minority within the Scottish electorate who are politically interested and well informed about the political situations in which their votes are cast. These voters are willing and able to make full use of the new electoral system in casting their votes. There is also a sizeable minority who continue to vote in the same way in which they always have, expressing loyalty to a party regardless of the political context or electoral system.

On the question of the electoral system, therefore, there is some evidence of a new politics emerging in Scotland. Certainly, there was clear majority support for the new electoral system, despite misgivings about some aspects of it. The new system – and no doubt the new institution as well – seems to have encouraged people to move away from their voting habits for Westminster elections. And there is evidence that a substantial group (one in five) of voters experimented with using the two ballots in different ways: a large enough group to have made a difference to the outcome.

NOTES

1. The regional votes were allocated by the constituencies that used to form the basis of elections to the European Parliament. Votes for each party were counted and divided by the number of constituency MSPs elected for each party, plus one. The party with most votes after this calculation gained the first additional member. The second to the seventh additional members were allocated in the same way, with additional members gained being included in the calculation.
2. These figures in Table 5.2 on non-voting are lower than for non-voting at the election and in our sample as a whole, because these items are drawn from the self-completion element of the survey. This element was more likely to be completed by those with a greater degree of political interest than the sample as a whole. Although this affects overall levels of reported voting and non-voting it should not affect the relationship between understanding of the system and turnout shown here. For further details of the surveys, see the Appendix.

6

HAS DEVOLUTION SAVED
THE UNION?

———·····‹····›·····———

INTRODUCTION

This chapter examines whether Scottish devolution has prolonged
the life of a united Britain or whether it has fuelled the desire for
more radical constitutional change in the form of independence. Has
the Scottish Parliament boosted support for independence, with
devolved government increasing people's desire for further autonomy
and – ultimately – a separate Scotland? Or has it had the opposite effect
and taken some of the wind out of the independence movement's
sails?

The chapter is based largely upon data from three surveys, the first
carried out immediately after the general election in spring 1997, the
second after the referendum later that same year, and the third after
the elections to the Scottish Parliament in spring 1999. (Further
details of these surveys can be found in the Appendix.)

We begin by examining people's views about how Scotland should
be governed and how these views have changed over time. This
allows us to assess the early impact of devolution upon people's constitutional preferences. Has support for independence been bolstered
by the advent of the Scottish Parliament? To what extent does the
public support the new status quo – a devolved parliament with

tax-varying powers? And is there any desire for a return to Scotland's pre-1999 relationship with the United Kingdom? We then examine how the views of particular groups have changed (or not), focusing particularly upon the young and the supporters of particular political parties. How, for instance, have the views about devolution held by Conservatives changed over time? Is there any sign that they have become more accepting of a parliament? Finally, we examine people's expectations of the Scottish Parliament – how these have changed over time and how they relate to attitudes towards devolution and independence. Are, for example, the highest expectations of the parliament held by those who would opt for an independent Scotland – or is it supporters of devolution who expect the most? It may be, for instance, that high expectations are linked with a general belief in Scotland's ability to manage its own affairs, in which case we might expect those favouring independence to be the most optimistic. Alternatively, however, optimism might relate to the particular form of government now in operation in Scotland, which would lead us to expect the pro-devolution group to be the most hopeful about the future.

CONSTITUTIONAL PREFERENCES

How have attitudes towards Scotland's possible constitutional future changed in the recent past? Certainly, throughout the late 1990s, support for a devolved parliament was higher than either support for the then status quo, or for independence, and by 1999 just over half supported a devolved parliament with tax-varying powers. Over the same period, support for independence remained remarkably stable, accounting for around a quarter of people. True, there was a change in opinion immediately after the referendum, with support for independence rising to account for over one-third of the population. However, support subsequently fell by ten percentage points which meant that, in the aftermath of the elections to the Scottish Parliament, it stood at the same level it enjoyed after the 1997 general election. Based on this evidence, then, devolution shows no sign of having boosted support for independence.

As Table 6.1 shows, support for a devolved parliament with tax-varying powers increased by 19 percentage points between the 1997 Referendum and 1999. Meanwhile, support for maintaining the Union with no Scottish Parliament whatsoever decreased sub-stantially, representing around one in six people in 1997 but only one in ten by 1999.

Table 6.1 Constitutional preferences, 1997–1999

	General Election 1997	Scottish Referendum 1997	Scottish Parliament election 1999
Independent from the UK	26	37	26
In UK with a Scottish Parliament with tax-varying powers	42	32	51
In UK with a Scottish Parliament with no tax-varying powers	9	9	9
In UK with no Scottish Parliament	17	17	10
Sample size (=100%)	841	676	1,427

Sources: Scottish Election Survey 1997; Scottish Referendum Survey 1997; Scottish Parliamentary Election Survey 1999

Not surprisingly, attitudes towards independence and devolution are closely linked to party political identification. We turn now to examine how this trend of increasing support for devolution (and decreasing support for independence) has affected party identifiers. As Table 6.2 shows, during the time that elapsed between the 1997 general election and the elections to the Scottish Parliament, support

Table 6.2 Support for a devolved parliament with tax-varying powers by party political identification, 1997–1999

Percentage support	General Election 1997	Sample size (=100%)	Scottish Parliament election 1999	Sample size (=100%)	Change 1997–1999
Party identification					
Conservative	25	142	43	221	+18
Labour	51	398	61	608	+10
Liberal Democrat	56	92	60	164	+4
Scottish National Party	28	138	32	279	+4
All	42	841	51	1,427	+9

Sources: Scottish Election Survey 1997; Scottish Parliamentary Election Survey 1999

for devolution grew among the supporters of all political parties, particularly Labour and Conservative identifiers. The largest change was found among the latter group who, despite remaining the *least* in favour of devolution, in 1999 included over two in five who would opt for a devolved parliament with tax-raising powers.

Only a minority of Conservatives (fewer than one-third) favour rejecting devolution altogether and returning to Scotland's previous relationship with the UK. This marks a substantial change in the position held in the aftermath of the 1997 general election (when it accounted for nearly half of Conservatives). The acceptance of devolution by the Conservative Party appears to be mirrored by its increasing acceptance among its supporters, perhaps heralding a gradual process of re-entry into mainstream Scottish politics.

**Table 6.3 Support for no parliament by party political
identification, 1997–1999**

Percentage support	General Election 1997	Sample size (=100%)	Scottish Parliament election 1999	Sample size (=100%)	Change 1997–1999
Party identification					
Conservative	48	142	29	221	−19
Labour	11	398	6	608	−5
Liberal Democrat	13	92	13	164	0
Scottish National Party	2	138	★	279	−2
All	17	841	10	1,427	−7

★ less than 1
Sources: Scottish Election Survey 1997; Scottish Parliamentary Election Survey 1999

Not surprisingly, SNP identifiers are consistently the most supportive of independence, and Conservative and Liberal Democrats the least. There was little change in views between the 1997 general election and the elections to the Scottish Parliament.

Attitudes towards Scotland's constitutional future have changed among other groups. As discussed in Chapter 7 (Table 7.6), support for devolution has grown even among those who see themselves as having a 'British' national identity (rather than a Scottish one). Shifting patterns of support are also evident among different religious groups. In 1997, immediately after the general election, Catholics were more enthusiastic about devolution than either those belonging to the Church of Scotland or those of no religious persuasion (Rosie and McCrone 2000). Members of both religious groups were substantially less likely than the non-religious to favour independence. By 1999, however, Catholics and the non-religious were equally in favour of independence (this accounting for roughly three in ten) – leaving Church of Scotland members lagging some way behind in their enthusiasm.

Table 6.4 Attitudes towards Scottish Parliament by religion

	All	No religion	Church of Scotland	Roman Catholic
Independent from the UK	26	30(–6)	21(+2)	32(+15)
In UK with a Scottish Parliament with tax-varying powers	51	49(+8)	53(+10)	52(+2)
In UK with no Scottish Parliament	10	9(–3)	10(–14)	8(–4)
Sample size (=100%)	1427	556	507	205

Change since general election 1997 in brackets.
Sources: Scottish Election Survey 1997; Scottish Parliamentary Election Survey 1999

There are also considerable age differences in attitudes towards independence and devolution. As Table 6.5 shows, support for independence falls significantly as we move up the age range, accounting for twice as many 18–24 year olds as those in the 55-plus age group. In fact, this youngest group is the only one which considers independence and devolution (in its current format) as more or less

Table 6.5 Constitutional preferences by age

	18–24	25–34	35–44	45–54	55–64	65+
Independent from the UK	43	29	29	26	22	17
In UK with a Scottish Parliament with tax-varying powers	40	49	50	50	55	58
In UK with a Scottish Parliament with no tax-varying powers	5	8	9	9	8	10
In UK with no Scottish Parliament	4	9	8	10	12	11
Sample size (=100%)	84	282	248	241	209	354

Source: Scottish Parliamentary Election Survey 1999

equally desirable. For all other age groups, devolution is considerably more attractive than independence. Only a small minority favour reverting back to a pre-devolution settlement, though this minority is markedly smaller among 18–24 year olds than among older groups. Moreover, since 1997, support for devolution increased among all age groups, with the exception of 18–24 year olds (Table 6.6).

Table 6.6 Support for a devolved parliament with tax-varying powers by age, 1997–1999

Percentage support	General Election 1997	Sample size (=100%)	Scottish Parliament election 1999	Sample size (=100%)	Change 1997–1999
18–24	41	73	40	84	−1
25–34	44	154	49	282	+5
35–44	39	147	50	248	+11
45–54	43	144	50	241	+7
55–64	48	122	55	209	+7
65+	40	192	58	354	+18
All	42	841	51	1,427	+9

Sources: Scottish Election Survey 1997; Scottish Parliamentary Election Survey 1999

The growing acceptability of devolution makes it unsurprising that few wish to see the Parliament abolished, and over half think that it should be given more powers. As Table 6.7 shows, the vast majority of those who favour independence think the Parliament should have more powers, as do about half of those who favour devolution. Few

Table 6.7 Attitudes towards Scottish Parliament by constitutional preference

Percentage agreeing	All	Independence	Devolution	No parliament
The Scottish Parliament should be abolished	11	4	5	71
The Scottish Parliament should be given more powers	56	83	53	15
Sample size (=100%)	1,427	372	739	122

Sources: Scottish Parliamentary Election Survey 1999

of these groups think the Parliament should be abolished (unlike those who would rather there was no parliament at all). Conservatives are the least likely to think that the Parliament should be granted new powers, only around a quarter (24 per cent) doing so. By contrast, nearly nine in ten (87 per cent) of SNP identifiers would like to extend the Parliament's powers.

So far then, the early signs suggest that, rather than scuppering the Union, devolution may well have contributed towards its salvation, at least in the short term. Across the political spectrum support for devolution increased in the run-up to the elections for the Scottish Parliament, and demand for independence remained static. There is, however, evidence of a desire to increase the autonomy of the Parliament by granting it further powers. There is very little desire to return to Scotland's previous constitutional relationship with the United Kingdom, even among Conservatives. While independence is not off the agenda, a return to Scotland's previous relationship with the UK certainly appears to be.

THE LIKELIHOOD OF INDEPENDENCE

What impact has devolution had on the perceived likelihood of independence? Do those who would rather have a devolved parliament see independence as less likely than those who would opt for independence as their first choice? To assess this the Scottish Parliamentary Election Survey asked:

> At any time in the next twenty years, do you think it is likely or unlikely that Scotland will become completely independent from the United Kingdom?

In 1999 just over half (51 per cent) thought independence to be 'quite' or 'very' likely within the next twenty years, more than did so immediately after the 1997 general election (42 per cent), but fewer than did so after the 1997 referendum (60 per cent). In this sense, then, devolution appears to have made the perceived likelihood of independence *less* likely.

Perhaps not surprisingly, those who favour independence are the most likely to expect it, three-quarters doing so. Those who would prefer a devolved parliament, or no parliament at all, are far less likely to think it is a realistic option within the next twenty years. (This said, over four in ten of those who would *not* opt for independence nevertheless think that it is likely.) And, while the expectations of those favouring independence have remained unchanged since the referendum in 1997, among other groups independence is now considered to be less likely than it was. This is particularly true of those who would rather there was no Scottish Parliament at all (although due to the small size of this group the change over time is not statistically significant). Perhaps, for them, devolution in practice appears less of a threat than it did in abstract, particularly when it comes to the possibility of its being a staging-post *en route* to independence.

Table 6.8 Expectations of likelihood of independence in next twenty years by constitutional preference, 1997–1999

Percentage expecting independence	Scottish Referendum 1997	Sample size (=100%)	Scottish Parliament election 1999	Sample size (=100%)	Change 1997–1999
Constitutional preference					
Independence	76	232	75	372	−1
Devolution	48	227	43	739	−5
No parliament	54	126	43	122	−11
All	58	676	51	1,427	−7

Sources: Scottish Election Survey 1997; Scottish Parliamentary Election Survey 1999

We have seen that the expectation of independence is highest among those who favour it, and as a result expectations are highest among SNP supporters and younger age groups. And again we find that among these groups the proportion expecting independence has hardly decreased at all since the referendum (despite an overall fall among the population as a whole). Among 18–24 year olds, for example, around two-thirds think independence likely in the next twenty years – 65 per cent after the referendum and 64 per cent after the election to the Scottish Parliament.

Of course, it is possible that changing attitudes towards the likelihood of Scottish independence are not related to the advent of devolution at all. To assess the relationship between the two the 1999 survey asked:

Which of the following comes closest to your views about a Scottish parliament? A Scottish Parliament will . . . make it more likely that Scotland eventually leaves the United Kingdom, make it more likely that Scotland stays in the United Kingdom, or make no difference at all?

The results are in Table 6.9. Just over a third of people think the Scottish Parliament makes the break-up of the Union more likely and three in ten think it makes no difference. Just over a quarter think it makes it less likely, up eight points since the 1997 referendum. Thus only a minority consider devolution to have actively contributed to the dissolution of the Union; devolution can hardly be seen to be fanning the flames of independence.

Table 6.9 Views on impact of Scottish Parliament on Scotland leaving the UK, 1997–1999

	Scottish Referendum 1997	Scottish Parliament election 1999	Change 1997–1999
Makes it more likely	42	37	−5
Makes no difference	32	31	−2
Makes it less likely	19	27	+8
Sample size (=100%)	676	1,427	

Sources: Scottish Referendum Survey 1997; Scottish Parliamentary Election Survey 1999

So far we have seen that, immediately after the election to the Scottish Parliament, half the population thought that independence was likely in the next twenty years, and four in ten considered devolution to have made this more likely than it had been. And yet in 1999 three-quarters of people did not opt for an independent Scotland as their first choice. How, then, do people feel about the prospect of independence – would independence be a good or a bad thing? When the question is posed in these terms, opinion is evenly divided, with 44 per cent seeing independence as a good thing, and 45 per cent as a bad one: see Table 6.10. So independence, though the first choice of a minority, is now viewed with equanimity by roughly half of those expressing a view. However, if we turn specifically to those who would rather devolution than independence, only one-third see independence as being a good thing (as did only one in ten of those who would rather have no Scottish Parliament).

Table 6.10 Views on Scottish independence by constitutional preference

	All	Independence	Devolution	No parliament
Very bad thing	14	1	13	49
Bad thing	31	7	42	41
Good thing	32	53	28	4
Very good thing	12	34	4	3
Sample size (=100%)	1,427	372	739	122

The question was: 'If Scotland did become independent some time in the future, do you think that this would be a bad thing or good thing?'
Source: Scottish Parliamentary Election Survey 1999

So far we have seen that the run-up to devolution was marked by an increase in support for a devolved parliament, and a fall in support for either independence or a return to the pre-devolutionary settlement. There has been a slight fall in the belief that independence is likely in the near future. However, independence remains firmly on the public agenda, particularly among younger age groups. Though independence might not be everyone's first choice for Scotland's future, this does not necessarily translate into a belief that it is an option that lies beyond the pale.

EXPECTATIONS OF THE SCOTTISH PARLIAMENT

It seems axiomatic that preferences regarding Scotland's future will be related to the perceived performance of the Scottish Parliament, whether successful or flawed. As the 1999 survey took place immediately after the election to the Scottish Parliament, it was of course not possible to examine people's views about how well it was functioning. Rather, here we examined people's optimism or pessimism about the Parliament and assessed how expectations have changed (or not) over time.

We began by examining people's attitudes towards the power and influence of the Scottish Parliament. At the time when the Parliament came into existence, how did people think power would be shared between it and Westminster when it came to Scottish matters? As Table 6.11 shows, similar proportions (around four in ten) thought the Scottish Parliament and Westminster would have the most influence. But this was clearly viewed with some scepticism – when it came to which *should* have the most influence, three-quarters thought it should be the Scottish Parliament.

Table 6.11 Views on relative influence of Scottish, UK and European Parliaments

	Will have most influence	*Should have most influence*
Scottish Parliament	42	74
UK Parliament	39	13
Local councils	8	8
European Union	5	1
Sample size (=100%)	1,427	1,427

Questions were: 'Who will have the most influence over the way Scotland is run once the Scottish Parliament starts work?' and the same with 'Who should . . .'.
Source: Scottish Parliamentary Election Survey 1999

This discrepancy between beliefs about which institution will, and which should, have the most influence over the way Scotland runs partly stems from a fundamental mistrust in the extent to which the UK government can serve Scottish interests, a well-established feature of Scottish opinion (see, for example, Paterson 1991: 115). Consequently, when asked to respond to the question 'How much do you trust the UK government to work in Scotland's best long-term interests?', one-third (32 per cent) said 'just about always' or 'most of the time': see Table 6.12. When asked the same question about a *Scottish* Parliament, an overwhelming majority (81 per cent) agreed. However, trust in a Scottish Parliament in this respect has fallen slightly over the past few years, from one-third taking the most trusting view in 1997 to one-quarter in 1999.

Levels of trust in the Scottish Parliament do not vary markedly between those identifying with different parties (Table 6.13), the exception being Conservatives (who remain the least trusting). However, the proportion of Conservatives taking the most trusting view of the Parliament increased between 1997 and 1999 – the only

Table 6.12 Trust in Scottish Parliament, 1997–1999

	Scottish Referendum 1997	Scottish Parliament election 1999	Change 1997–1999
Trust Scottish Parliament to 'work in Scotland's best interests'			
Just about always	36	26	−10
Most of the time	48	55	+7
Only some of the time/ almost never	15	16	+1
Sample size (=100%)	676	1,427	

Sources: Scottish Referendum Survey 1997; Scottish Parliamentary Election Survey 1999

group among whom this happened. Seven in ten (71 per cent) of this group now trust the Scottish Parliament to work in Scotland's best interests at least most of the time, another indication of the Conservatives' increasing acceptance of devolution.

Table 6.13 Trust in Scottish Parliament by party political identification, 1997–1999

Percentage who trust Scottish Parliament to work in Scotland's best interests 'just about always'	Scottish Referendum 1997	Sample size (=100%)	Scottish Parliament election 1999	Sample size (=100%)	Change 1997–1999
Party identification					
Conservative	12	123	18	221	+6
Labour	42	336	27	608	−15
Liberal Democrat	39	51	29	164	−10
Scottish National Party	46	122	32	279	−14
All	36	676	26	1,427	−10

Sources: Scottish Referendum Survey 1997; Scottish Parliamentary Election Survey 1999

So far we have seen that, despite a slight fall in people's faith in the Scottish Parliament acting in the country's best interests, there is vastly more trust in the Scottish Parliament being able to do this than in the UK one. But we have also seen a certain amount of cynicism about the autonomy of the Scottish Parliament and its ability to break free from Westminster. That said, seven in ten think the Parliament will give Scotland a stronger voice in the UK, exactly the same proportion as thought this immediately after the 1997 referendum (Table 6.14). However, over the same period there has been a marked decrease in the proportion who believe that the Parliament will give 'ordinary Scottish people' more of a say in how Scotland is governed. These high expectations, and the tendency for them to have been dampened down somewhat in the run-up to devolution, are even more apparent when we consider people's views about the impact of the Parliament's policies. For instance, the proportion thinking the Parliament would increase standards of education in Scotland fell considerably (though over half still thought that it would improve standards), as did the proportion thinking it would increase living standards. In all cases, however, this fall in optimism was accounted for by a rise in the proportion saying that the Parliament would make no difference (and was not due to people thinking that the Parliament would make things worse).

Table 6.14 Expectations of Scottish Parliament, 1997–1999

Percentage agreeing	Scottish Referendum 1997	Scottish Parliament election 1999	Change 1997–1999
Will give Scotland a stronger voice in the United Kingdom	70	71	+1
Will give ordinary Scottish people more say in how Scotland is governed	79	64	−15
Will increase standards of education	71	56	−15
Will increase standards of living in Scotland	50	38	−12
Sample size (=100%)	676	1,427	

Sources: Scottish Referendum Survey 1997; Scottish Parliamentary Election Survey 1999

This lowering of expectations is perhaps not surprising. After all, in the aftermath of the 1997 referendum, people's beliefs about what a parliament could deliver may have been overly optimistic. It may be, therefore, that the run-up to the 1999 elections were simply marked by the restoration of a more realistic view about what the Parliament could, and could not, achieve. However, Table 6.15 shows that the same dampening-down of expectations is also apparent if we compare expectations in 1999 with those held after the 1997 general election (when we would not expect them to be so high). Between these dates the proportions thinking that the Parliament would result in lower unemployment and a better health service and economy all fell. However, nearly half still expect the Parliament to improve the standard of the NHS in Scotland, and a similar proportion think that it will have a beneficial effect on Scotland's economy.

Table 6.15 Expectations of Scottish Parliament, 1997–1999

Percentage agreeing	General Election 1997	Scottish Parliament election 1999	Change 1997–1999
Unemployment in Scotland will become lower	37	28	−9
Scotland's economy will become better	54	43	−11
The standard of the health service in Scotland will become better	60	50	−10
Sample size (=100%)	841	1,427	

Sources: Scottish Election Survey 1997; Scottish Parliamentary Election Survey 1999

People's expectations, and the extent to which they fell in the run-up to devolution, varied according to party identification (Table 6.16). Not surprisingly, Conservatives had the lowest expectations, and SNP identifiers the highest. However, while the expectations of SNP identifiers fell markedly between 1997 and 1999, those of Conservatives remained stable (although at a very low level). In many respects, Conservatives remain unconvinced so far about the benefits of devolution. In particular, the proportion thinking that it will have a negative effect on unemployment or Scotland's economy substantially outweighs those taking a more positive view. Thus while 15 per cent in 1999 thought that unemployment would fall under devolution, nearly double (27 per cent) thought that it would increase. And, though 18 per cent thought that Scotland's economy would improve,

32 per cent think that it would suffer. It seems that the first years of devolution will be critical in convincing this group about the merits (or otherwise) of a Scottish Parliament.

Table 6.16 Views about impact of Scottish Parliament on Scottish economy by party identification, 1997–1999

Percentage expecting Parliament to improve economy	General Election 1997	Sample size (=100%)	Scottish Parliament election 1999	Sample size (=100%)	Change 1997–1999
Party identification					
Conservative	21	142	18	221	−3
Labour	60	398	47	608	−13
Liberal Democrat	42	92	38	164	−4 .
SNP	81	138	60	279	−19
All	54	841	43	1,427	−11

Sources: Scottish Election Survey 1997; Scottish Parliamentary Election Survey 1999

In some cases, optimism about the efficacy of the Parliament varies with age. The youngest are the most optimistic about the ability of the Parliament to improve Scotland's economy and result in increased standards of living. But their views about the impact of the Parliament on education, unemployment and the NHS are not notably different from those held by other groups. Nor is there any clear pattern in the way that the attitudes of different age groups have changed over time.

Expectations of devolution are also related to people's constitutional preferences (Table 6.17). But the highest expectations are not held by those favouring devolution – rather, they are found among those who would prefer Scotland to be independent altogether. In 1999, one in two of this group thought the Parliament would improve standards of living, as did four in ten of those favouring a devolved parliament with tax-varying powers and only one in fourteen of those who would rather there was no devolution. A similar pattern exists for all the measures of expectations we have considered so far. In most cases, only around one in ten of those who would rather there was no parliament thought that the Parliament would improve matters. However, when it came to education and standards in the health service, even in this group around a quarter thought the Parliament would have a beneficial impact.

The expectations of both the pro-independence and pro-devolution groups fell between 1997 and 1999. For instance, the proportion of those favouring independence who thought a Scottish Parliament would improve living standards in Scotland fell seventeen points, with a comparable fall of twenty-two points among those who favoured devolved government. There was little change among the group who would rather there was no parliament, largely because so few expected it to be able to deliver improved standards of living in the first place.

Table 6.17   Views about impact of Scottish Parliament on standards of living in Scotland by constitutional preference, 1997–1999

Percentage expecting Parliament to improve standards of living	Scottish Referendum 1997	Sample size (=100%)	Scottish Parliament election 1999	Sample size (=100%)	Change 1997–1999
Constitutional preference					
Independence	68	232	51	372	−17
Devolution	62	227	40	739	−22
No parliament	9	126	7	122	−2
All	50	676	38	1,427	−12

Sources: Scottish Referendum Survey 1997; Scottish Parliamentary Election Survey 1999

What might falling expectations mean for the Parliament? The dampening-down of enthusiasm in the run-up to devolution may well be good news for it. Perhaps people's initial expectations (especially in the aftermath of the referendum) were unduly idealistic and have simply become more realistic over time. If this is true, the Parliament should find it easier to live up to people's expectations than it would have done otherwise. A less rosy interpretation, at least so far as the Parliament is concerned, is that falling expectations merely reflect the first signs of public disillusionment with the Parliament's abilities. (These points are discussed further by Paterson (2000a).)

CONCLUSION

At the time of writing, the Scottish Parliament had been in existence for just over a year. Its future, and that of the Union, will be decided over a far greater time-period than this. Nevertheless, we have attempted here to assess the initial impact of devolution on public opinion, and identify some of the issues which might be relevant in influencing views about Scotland's future.

In terms of people's constitutional preferences – whether they would rather an independent Scotland, a devolved parliament, or no parliament at all – the immediate impact of devolution has been increased support for it, alongside a belief that the Parliament should be given more powers. Meanwhile, support for independence has remained stable. Clearest of all is the fact that there is very little support for a return to Scotland's previous relationship with the United Kingdom. Even among Conservatives, this is now a minority view.

This said, among the young, support for independence remains high, support for abolishing the Parliament is extremely low, and – unlike that of older groups – their enthusiasm for devolution itself did not increase in the run-up to the devolved parliament. It remains to be seen whether this generation will maintain these distinctive views as it ages.

Expectations about the effectiveness of the Scottish Parliament, in terms of its impact on democracy and the efficacy of its policies, fell in the run-up to devolution, reflecting what were perhaps unrealistically high expectations in the aftermath of the 1997 referendum. Increased pessimism was apparent across the majority of the population, but was less marked among people who opted for no parliament (largely because their expectations were lowest to begin with). But despite decreasing optimism about the efficacy of the Parliament, expectations remained relatively high.

Might the Parliament, if it is perceived to perform well, stave off demands for independence? We find little evidence to support this view. Expectations about the Parliament are highest among those who support independence, suggesting that optimism reflects a belief in Scotland's ability to manage its own affairs rather than a conviction that the best way to do this is through a devolved parliament. Consequently, if the Parliament is seen to do well, then it is by no means clear that demands for independence will diminish.

Of course, in reality, opinion about the Parliament's performance is likely to be less fulsome. For example, an ICM/*Scotsman* poll in September 2000 reported that only 11 per cent of people thought the Scottish Parliament had achieved 'a lot', 56 per cent thought it had achieved 'a little', and 29 per cent thought it had achieved nothing. It remains to be seen what impact more detailed assessments of the Parliament will have on attitudes to independence, but it is clear that it remains firmly on the public agenda. Devolution in itself will not save the Union. But it is clear that its future will depend, at least to a large extent, on how the parliaments in Scotland as well as in Westminster are perceived to perform in the long run.

7

THE POLITICS OF
NATIONAL IDENTITY

---~~~RR☉RR~~~---

INTRODUCTION

Issues of national identity have been at the forefront of Scottish politics, notably during the last two decades or so. The importance of a
Scottish agenda has clearly grown, most obviously in the demand for
and creation of a Scottish parliament in 1999. It would seem fairly
self-evident that the first elections to the new parliament have been
fuelled by assertions of Scottish identity. This chapter explores the
extent to which there has been a firming up of Scottish identity in
the past two decades, as well as the impact on political and constitutional opinion. In particular, we examine the extent to which the
electorate now feels more exclusively Scottish than previously; the
extent to which having a devolved parliament amplifies or reduces
this sense of Scottishness; and whether defining oneself as Scottish or
British makes a difference to the constitutional future which people
prefer. In short, is Scotland's 'new politics' driven by a growing sense
of Scottish national identity?

IDENTITY AND CONSTITUTIONAL CHANGE

The relationship between how people perceive their national identity
and their attitudes to constitutional change is complex. Thus, we

might expect those who have a strong sense of being Scottish to push for constitutional change, while those who think of themselves as British prefer the status quo. On the other hand, it could well be that being in favour of a Scottish parliament predisposes people to think of themselves as Scottish, so that constitutional preference has an impact on national identity. Be that as it may, we might well expect that the heightened political climate of the last few years has helped to generate a stronger sense of Scottishness, that, whatever the causal connections are, people voting in the first Scottish parliamentary election in 1999 would articulate strong feelings of national identity.

We know from analysis of the 1997 election and referendum surveys that Scottish national identity in itself did not explain support for a Scottish parliament in the 1997 referendum. By this we mean that how individuals described themselves – their personal identity – did not divide the population into pro- and anti-home rule groupings. While it was true that those who felt more Scottish were more likely to vote yes (62 per cent), it was also true that those who thought of themselves as British also supported a parliament, albeit to a lesser degree (50 per cent) (Brown *et al.* 1999: 126). Similarly, in Chapter 4 above (Table 4.8) we find that national identity is a weak predictor of vote in the election for the first Scottish parliament. One interpretation of these findings, which we explore in this chapter, is that national identity does not in and of itself explain constitutional and political attitudes. This is not because it is unimportant, but because it is pervasive, colouring how politics operates in Scotland, and is thus shared by those with different political and constitutional beliefs.

While national identity in Scotland does seem part of the taken-for-granted world, it is not an easy concept to measure. We cannot be sure, for example, that two people who say they are Scottish mean the same thing. In like manner, we cannot assume that being Scottish and being British are antithetical. Indeed, for much of post-Union history, it seems that they were largely complementary (Morton 1999), so that one's national identity was Scottish, but state identity British. Since the mid-1980s, we have made use of the question first applied by Luis Moreno (and called the Moreno scale simply as a form of shorthand) to measure how people relate being Scottish and being British, if at all. The technique had been used in mass surveys in Spain in 1979 (Gunther *et al.* 1986), and was adapted by Moreno for use in Scotland (Moreno 1988). This survey was administered to a sample of people living in Scotland, and not simply to people who defined themselves as Scots. Thus, given that around 10 per cent of people living in Scotland were born elsewhere, and that the Scots-born who live outside Scotland are excluded from the Scottish sample, the sample seeks to reflect the population in Scotland. The question takes the form:

> Which, if any, of the following best describes how you see yourself?
> Scottish, not British
> More Scottish than British
> Equally Scottish and British
> More British than Scottish
> British, not Scottish
> None of these

In surveys of this type we have the problem of knowing what people themselves mean by the terms with which they are presented. The question is in the form of a scale, ranging between single identities, either Scottish or British, at either end, with a mid-point where they are equal, and points 2 and 4 where one or other is stressed but both are included. We should bear in mind that this scale represents a continuum such that respondents are required to choose a fixed item which corresponds most closely with their position, and not to mark themselves on a point on a linear scale. This practice makes comparing responses easier for analytical purposes, although it has the potential for missing the exact place in which respondents would put themselves.

The second survey measure we have used is a simpler question which asks respondents to opt for which, from a range, best describes their identity. They are asked:

> If you had to choose, which one best describes the way you think of yourself?
> British
> English
> European
> Irish
> Northern Irish
> Scottish
> Welsh
> None of these

The point of this simpler measure is that it forces people to choose, not because that's the way life is, but for methodological purposes, so that we can test hypotheses on the impact of identities. Thus, for example, we might expect 'Scots' to favour constitutional change, whereas those who are 'British' do not. None of this is to deny that, in practice, identities are much more fluid and multiple in that people have a fair degree of choice in deciding how they wish to present themselves in different contexts and for different purposes. In a cross-sectional survey of the sort we are using here, however, that level of complexity and nuance is not available to us, although in this chapter we will explore some data on how the same people respond at different points in time so that we get some idea of the stability or otherwise of national identity.

In general terms, the focus on national identity allows us to test its relationship with constitutional change. Thus we might expect that the creation of a Scottish parliament might heighten a sense of being Scottish such that in due course there is a ratchet effect. The more Scottish people feel, the more they expect of a parliament, leading, as the SNP might hope and the Conservatives fear, to ultimate independence. There is, of course, an alternative hypothesis, which the current Labour/Liberal Democrat Scottish coalition government hopes for, namely that, now a parliament has been set up, there is less need to emphasise Scottishness. After all, they argue, was there not a heightened sense of Scottishness during the late 1980s when there was a Thatcher government? Now that there is a Labour government in London, and the Scottish Parliament in Edinburgh, people can be more relaxed about multiple identities, being Scottish but British as well. Just as people in Catalonia appear to be increasingly relaxed about their Spanishness (Moreno and Arriba 1996), then surely Scots can be happy about being British? While it is early days in the life of the Parliament to say much about the long-term effects, the survey does give us the opportunity to test these alternative hypotheses, which, by way of shorthand, we will call the ratchet effect and the dampening effect.

CHANGING IDENTITIES

Let us begin by a simple examination of change over time. Here, we focus on five major surveys, which were conducted using similar methods: the election surveys of 1979, 1992 and 1997, whose sample sizes were enhanced in Scotland to provide analytically useful and comparative data; the survey carried out shortly after the referendum in September 1997; and, the focus of this book, the Scottish Parliamentary Election Survey of 1999. Details of these appear in the Appendix.

Table 7.1 shows two sets of data – the first two categories on 'Moreno' as a measure of Scottishness: that is, those who say they are Scottish not British, and more Scottish than British; and the second, in the lower half of the table, forced-choice best identity. Whichever way we look at it, there appears to have been a strengthening of Scottish identity. Although the question was not asked in 1979, we see that by 1999, fully two-thirds of respondents prioritise being Scottish over being British (either Scottish not British, or more Scottish than British). The modal position in 1999 was 'more Scottish than British', with 22 per cent equally Scottish and British, and only 7 per cent either more British than Scottish, or British not Scottish, results broadly in line with previous surveys. We can see the change most dramatically in the 'forced-choice' categories. Whereas over one-third of respondents opted for 'British' in 1979, and over half 'Scottish', the 1980s saw what appears to be a long-term shift towards 'Scottish'. By 1992, only a quarter considered themselves 'British', and almost

Table 7.1 National identity, 1979–1999

Percentage choosing that identity	1979	1992	1997 General Election	1997 Referendum	1999
Scottish not British*	not asked	19	23	32	32
Scottish more than British*	not asked	40	38	32	35
Scottish**	56	72	72	85	77
British**	38	25	24	15	17
Sample size (=100%)	661	957	882	676	1,482

*Moreno question
**Forced-choice 'best' identity
Sources: Scottish Election Surveys of 1979, 1992 and 1997; Scottish Referendum Survey 1997; Scottish Parliamentary Election Survey 1999

three-quarters 'Scottish'. A further step-shift occurred in the Scotland-only event of the referendum. Those who prioritised being British were reduced to around one in six, whereas more than eight out of ten said they were Scottish.

The table suggests that the referendum provoked an intensification of Scottishness, and that this was maintained in the 1999 Scottish parliamentary election, for Scottishness did not fall back to previous levels, nor did Britishness rise accordingly. This is the first piece of evidence to suggest that constitutional change has broadly amplified rather than diminished Scottish national identity. While slightly fewer people than during the referendum say they are Scottish, the number remains above the figures for the earlier 1990s. Thus it seems that the Scottish parliamentary election, like the referendum in 1997, saw a strong assertion of Scottishness, possibly because both were uniquely 'Scottish' events, compared with the UK general election of 1997.

Cross-sectional surveys of this kind only give us snapshots as to how people see themselves at single time-points. We have as yet very little evidence as to how they might change their response over time. However, the British Election Panel Study, which is part of the British and Scottish Election Studies, does allow us to check on how the same people responded at different times, in this case, in 1997 and 1999. (More details about the Panel Study appear in the Appendix.) We can, of course, say little about the stimuli which caused them to respond in the ways they did, but this is a unique way of measuring how stable or fluid national categories are. In this respect, it is more sensible to use the 5-point scale in the 'Moreno' question rather than the blunt Scottish or British categories.

Table 7.2 shows that in the main categories (Scottish not British, more Scottish than British, and equally Scottish and British), there is both continuity and fluidity. Thus, 50 per cent say they are Scottish not British at both time-points, 52 per cent more Scottish than British, and 66 per cent equally Scottish and British. Of those who respond differently at the two time-points, most opt for an adjacent category. Thus, for each of the three main identity categories, there is a one-step change of 36 per cent, 44 per cent and 21 per cent respectively, with the greatest single change in the most extreme category, Scottish not British. What these results suggest is that there is a fair degree of stability as regards national identity among people in

Scotland. As regards the minority options of more British than Scottish, and British not Scottish, less than 3 per cent move into these 'British' categories from the 'Scottish' ones, indicating that while people in Scotland are not averse to being British also, they rarely accentuate their 'state' identity over their 'national' identity.

Table 7.2   Changes in national identity, 1997–1999

1999	1997				
	Sc not Br	Sc>Br	Sc=Br	Br>Sc or Br not Sc	All
Sc≠Br	50	18	11	4	22
Sc>Br	36	52	17	8	35
Sc=Br	8	26	66	31	33
Br>or≠Sc	2	3	4	50	7
Sample size (=100%)	146	251	148	45	590

Identity categories are Moreno: see text
Percentages do not add up to 100 because none/other/not applicable cases have been omitted
Source: British Election Panel Study 1997 and 1999

What influenced people to change their response between 1997 and 1999? We have examined a number of factors such as age, sex, social class, party identification, how they voted in the Scottish elections, people's views on taxation and spending, economic redistribution and pride in being Scottish. We could find no systematic social patterns involved, suggesting that no social group is especially prone to change its national identity over time, but that individuals adapt how they describe themselves according to particular contexts. So we can conclude that it would be erroneous to assume that national identity, like other forms of social identity, is a fixed quality, that it operates as a badge which people wear almost all of the time. National identity has been described as a 'banal' characteristic (Billig 1995) in that it is implicit and taken for granted much of the time. For certain groups (such as incomers) and on certain rare occasions (most obviously in times of war), national identity can be problematic or overwhelming. It appears from Table 7.2 that national 'identity' is rather more fluid than is commonly supposed, although not so variable that it does not

remain structured by broad allegiances (such as the persisting preference in Scotland for not giving greater allegiance to Britain than to
Scotland).

NATIONAL IDENTITY AND CLASS IDENTITY

What of the argument that it is the politics of social class rather than
the politics of national identity which matters? After all, the Labour
Party has been disproportionately strong in Scotland, as in Wales,
and some writers have interpreted the rise of nationalism simply as
a political expedient (Hobsbawm 1990), as a surrogate form of class
politics. However, we can see from Table 7.3 that what undoubtedly
has happened in the last twenty years is a shift from shared class
identity regardless of nationality, to one in which nationality pre-
dominates.

**Table 7.3 Relative importance of class and national identity,
1979–1999**

	1979	*1992*	*1997* *General* *Election*	*1997* *Referendum*	*1999*
Same–class English	44	27	23	25	24
Opposite-class Scots	38	45	46	38	43
Sample size (=100%)	483	957	882	676	1,415

Question: 'Would you say that you had more in common with (*same-class*) English people or with (*opposite-class*) Scottish people?' Interviewer inserted the class identity that
respondent had chosen in previous question which asked how respondent identified
himself/herself in class terms (as working or middle class).
Sources: Scottish Election Surveys of 1979, 1992 and 1997; Scottish Referendum Survey
1997; Scottish Parliamentary Election Survey 1999

We can see that in 1979 people in Scotland were marginally more
likely to put class above nationality, and that the major shift occurred
as early as the 1980s so that by the 1992 survey there was a consistent
identification with nationality above class such that it approached a
ratio of two to one. We even find those who think of themselves as
'British' identifying marginally more with other-class Scots than

same-class English (33 per cent to 30 per cent). Scottish identifiers are more than twice as likely to do so (45 per cent to 21 per cent).

That nationality is preferred to class is reflected among middle-class as well as working-class respondents, both in terms of occupational class and self-ascribed class. People in Scotland are more likely to think of themselves as working class despite their class of origin and own social class. The overall proportions assigning themselves to working class are 59 per cent in England and Wales, and 71 per cent in Scotland. This difference is entirely explained by a greater propensity of people who are upwardly mobile from working class to middle class to say that they are actually working class: 80 per cent of such people in Scotland, and 65 per cent in England. The 1999 survey found that a majority identified with opposite-class Scots among both people who call themselves working class and among people who call themselves middle class.

NATIONAL IDENTITY AND VOTE

Our next task is to set national identity in a political context. How people vote and how they see themselves in terms of their national identity are likely to be related. For example, at either end of the constitutional question, we might assume that SNP voters are self-defined Scots, and Tories self-defined British. However, the situation is both more complicated, and more intriguing, than that. In Table 7.4 we explore how voters who identify with a particular party see themselves in terms of national identity. If we look at change over time, we see some vital changes in the relationship between vote and identity. Table 7.4 shows the levels of Scottishness and of Britishness among people who identify with particular parties: for example, the figure of 46 per cent in the top left-hand corner means that of people who saw themselves as Conservatives in 1979, 46 per cent called themselves Scottish.

In the first place, we see a shift over time towards Scottishness among voters of all parties, including Conservatives. Thus, while Tories split 46/48 in terms of Scottish/British in 1979, twenty years later it was 61/35. Scanning the time-frames, we can see a steady percentage point increase in all parties in opting to self-define as Scottish: from eighteen percentage points among Liberal Democrats, seventeen for Labour, fifteen for Conservatives, and even nine points

Table 7.4 National identity by party identification, 1979–1999

Percentage choosing that identity among supporters of named party	1979	1992	1997 General Election	1997 Referendum	1999
Scottish★					
Conservative	46	58	56	68	61
Labour	60	74	75	89	77
Liberal Democrat	52	64	63	78	70
SNP	84	90	93	94	93
British★					
Conservative	48	38	39	32	35
Labour	36	23	22	11	16
Liberal Democrat	39	31	32	20	17
SNP	9	10	5	5	5

★Forced-choice 'best' identity
Sample sizes (=100%): 1979 – Cons 205, Lab 245, LD 64, SNP 68; 1992 – Con 250, Lab 332, LD 67, SNP 186; 1997 general election – Cons 144, Lab 415, LD 96, SNP 147; 1997 referendum – Cons 123, Lab 336, LD 51, SNP 122; 1999 – Cons 231, Lab 625, LD 166, SNP 290
Sources: Scottish Election Surveys of 1979, 1992 and 1997; Scottish Referendum Survey 1997; Scottish Parliamentary Election Survey 1999

among SNP identifiers, who, naturally, start from a much higher base than the other parties. In terms of being British, we see a concomitant decline: from twenty-two percentage points among Liberal Democrats, twenty for Labour, thirteen for Tories, and four for SNP voters. Looking at the data this way, we can conclude that the decline in Britishness has been most pronounced among Labour and Liberal Democrat identifiers, precisely those parties which champion a devolved parliament, and which comprise its coalition government.

There is another way of looking at the relationship between national identity and party identification. Table 7.5 is the opposite way round from Table 7.4, namely, the distribution of party identities among Scottish identifiers on the one hand, and British identifiers on the other.

What this table shows is that Labour has always commanded the majority allegiance of Scottish identifiers. Thus, in both 1979 and 1999, 41 per cent of 'Scots' are Labour supporters. Focusing still on

Table 7.5 Party identification by national identity, 1979–1999

Distribution of party identifiers among people of named identity	1979	1992	1997 General Election	1997 Referendum	1999
Scottish★					
Conservative	26	21	12	13	13
Labour	41	35	48	52	41
Liberal Democrat	9	6	10	7	11
SNP	16	24	22	22	25
Sample size (=100%)	365	690	645	572	1,136
British★					
Conservative	41	40	26	34	33
Labour	36	32	42	38	38
Liberal Democrat	10	9	16	11	12
SNP	3	8	4	6	6
Sample size (=100%)	242	239	177	101	252

★Forced-choice 'best' identity
Sources: Scottish Election Surveys of 1979, 1992 and 1997; Scottish Referendum Survey 1997; Scottish Parliamentary Election Survey 1999

Scottish identifiers, we can see that the Conservative share has halved (from 26 to 13 per cent), and that the SNP share has risen to one-quarter. Turning our attention to the 'British' identifiers, we see that Conservatives no longer command the majority allegiance, which has gone to Labour. Looking at these data in a slightly different way, it is clear that Labour and Liberal Democrat support is almost unrelated to national identity (Labour, for example, takes an almost equal share of both national groups: 41 per cent and 38 per cent). On the other hand, Conservative and SNP support is most strongly related to national identity, in inverse ways. What these data suggest is that the future of Scottish politics looks to be mainly in the hands of Labour voters. If they shift their allegiance to being Scottish, then it will perhaps be harder for a sense of Britishness to survive. If, however, Labour voters remain 'British' in any number, then we will see a continuing shift in the political meaning of the term, given that since 1979 it was largely the preserve of the Tories. Labour's dilemma is how to ride both horses at once. Labour may be forced to choose between a Scottish and a British identity. On the other hand, Labour also has the potential to bridge the divide between the two identities so as to stabilise the Union, a theme we explored in Chapter 6. Thus, the fact that Labour and the Liberal Democrats are cross-identity parties and form the coalition government places them in the centre of the Scottish–British nexus, and enables them to appeal to both the Scottish and the British identities that most voters hold to.

NATIONAL IDENTITY AND CONSTITUTIONAL PREFERENCE

We cannot, of course, make these calculations simply on the basis of national identity and party identification. Let us explore constitutional preference directly. Table 7.6, which is analogous to Table 7.5, shows the distribution of constitutional preferences among those identifying as Scottish or British. We can see in the first instance that a home rule parliament is preferred by both Scottish and British identifiers. We can therefore begin to understand just why there is a consensus about home-rule, for it does not act to partition the electorate by national identity. To put it another way, knowing whether someone thinks of themselves as Scottish or British is a poor predictor of their preferred constitutional option, and it is striking that both Scottish and British identifiers much prefer home rule – the new consensus – to any other option.

There is however a differential as regards independence. Not only has there been a growth among Scottish identifiers in support for independence (from 11 per cent in 1979 to 31 per cent twenty years later), but the independence option is almost three times stronger among Scottish identifiers than it is among those who define themselves as British. We should be careful, however, about drawing rash conclusions from this. Put simply, thinking of oneself as Scottish does not guarantee support for independence. After all, as many as 58 per cent of self-defining 'Scots' support home rule, not independence. We can also see from this table that there has been a sharp drop in support for no elected body, especially among British identifiers between the referendum of 1997 and the first parliamentary election

**Table 7.6 Constitutional preference by national identity,
1979–1999**

Distribution of constitutional preferences among people of named identity	date				
	1979	1992	1997 General Election	1997 Referendum	1999
Scottish★					
independence	11	27	32	41	31
home rule, devolution etc.	66	50	52	41	58
no elected body	23	20	12	13	6
Sample size (=100%)	365	690	645	572	1,136
British★					
independence	2	11	10	15	11
home rule, devolution etc.	58	48	51	39	62
no elected body	40	38	34	41	24
Sample size (=100%)	242	239	177	101	252

★Forced-choice 'best' identity
Sources: Scottish Election Surveys of 1979, 1992 and 1997; Scottish Referendum Survey 1997; Scottish Parliamentary Election Survey 1999

in 1999. This also reflects a coming to terms with the new parliament among Conservatives and others previously hostile to devolution.

That around a quarter of British identifiers in Table 7.6 still prefer no elected body is nicely confirmed by the similar figure (22 per cent) in Table 7.7 who think that the Scottish parliament should be abolished. This group probably represents the hard core of 'British Unionists' in Scotland who, while insufficiently large to directly influence affairs themselves, represent a key element of likely Conservative opinion.

What is interesting about these data is that they show a strong desire among both Scottish and British identifiers to make the Parliament work. There is also majority support among both groups for the view that the Scottish Parliament should be more important

113

Table 7.7 Attitudes to Scottish Parliament by national identity

Percentage agreeing	Scottish★	British★
Scottish Parliament should be abolished (agree or agree strongly)	8	22
Scottish Parliament should be made to work	98	97
Scottish Parliament should have more powers	62	33
Scottish Parliament ought to have more influence than Westminster	78	61
sample size (=100%)	1,136	252

★Forced-choice 'best' identity
Source: Scottish Parliamentary Election Survey 1999

than Westminster. On the other hand, Scottish identifiers are much more likely than British identifiers to want the Scottish Parliament to have more powers, confirming what we found in Chapter 6. This is at a much higher level (by as much as a factor of two) than support for independence (Table 7.6).

Leaving aside their preferences (which we also explored in Chapter 6), we can see from Table 7.8 that a majority of Scottish identifiers expect independence within twenty years, although fewer Scottish and British identifiers think this is likely to happen if we compare the 1997 referendum and 1999 election responses.

Table 7.8 Expectations of likelihood of independence in the next twenty years by national identity, 1997–1999

Percentage expecting independence	1997 Referendum	1999
Scottish★	62 (572)	55 (1,136)
British★	44 (101)	37 (252)

★ Forced-choice 'best' identity
sample sizes (=100%) in brackets
Sources: Scottish Referendum Survey 1997 and Scottish Parliamentary Election Survey 1999

What, at this point in our argument, can we conclude about national identity? If, for methodological purposes, we divide our sample into Scottish and British identifiers, we find that over three-quarters of people living in Scotland define themselves as Scottish, and only around one in six say that they are primarily British. This pattern of national identification is found among supporters of all political parties, but especially the home rule parties, Labour and Liberal Democrat, who formed the backbone of the constitutional convention, and now the coalition government. Devolution is a political project which spans the Scottish–British divide, and it is being run by a coalition government made up of parties spanning that divide. The success of these parties seems to rest on their ability to maintain and, if possible, strengthen this bridge position. The difficulty they have, however, is that the national divide is asymmetric, for far more people define themselves as Scottish than British (Table 7.1), and only 22 per cent claim to be equally Scottish and British. This implies that the Scottish Executive is under pressure to address Scottish rather than purely British issues, reinforced by the fact that devolution gives them a remit for Scottish matters. Neither Labour nor the Liberal Democrats depend on national identification for support to anything like the extent of the SNP and the Conservatives. Labour voters are now the core of the 'British' group, reflecting in part the falling-away of the Tories in Scotland. National identification is, in itself, a poor predictor of constitutional preference, although self-defined Scots are more likely than their British counterparts to argue that the Scottish Parliament should have more powers, and that it should have more influence than Westminster. Where a more powerful home-rule parliament stops and an independent one begins is unclear, although Scottish identifiers are more likely to expect independence to happen within twenty years.

This analysis shows that there is a complex relationship between party identification, constitutional preference and national identity in Scotland. Let us look first at SNP voters. Ninety-three per cent of them consider themselves to be 'Scottish', but only 61 per cent are in favour of independence. What of people who define themselves as Scottish? Only one-quarter of them vote for the SNP, and less than one-third (31 per cent) are in favour of independence. Finally, what about those who want an independent Scotland? Eighty-eight per cent of them think of themselves as Scottish, but only 45 per cent vote SNP. The fact that party choice, national identity and constitutional preference do not overlap in any neat way suggests that there are different ways of 'being Scottish'. When the SNP lays claim to be 'Scotland's party', this is highly contested by the other parties who

115

have strong claims of their own. This rather loose correspondence between ways of being Scottish permeates social and political life. One might say that national identity in Scotland is a poor predictor of vote and constitutional preference not because it is unimportant, but because it is all-pervasive, and not the property of any single political party.

THE IMPLICATIONS OF NATIONAL IDENTITY

If national identity is strengthening in Scotland, might we be seeing the development of a more 'exclusive' sense of Scottishness such that there is heightened feeling of Scottish–English conflict, as well as a desire for a more restrictive definition as to what counts as 'Scottish'? Media comment often highlights a growing sense of Scottishness as an explanation for a purported escalation in Scottish–English conflict, and it is a familiar theme in accounting for an increase in cases of discrimination brought to the Commission for Racial Equality. The image presented is often of a heightened 'ethnic' awareness in which incoming English people are subject to discrimination and abuse, generating a sense of an oppressed 'British' minority. Table 7.9 shows that there has indeed been an increase in the percentage thinking that conflict between Scotland and England is serious, the figure doubling between 1979 and 1992, and reaching 43 per cent by the end of the decade. This, at first glance, seems to confirm the view that, whatever the cause, the demand for home rule has coincided with increased tension.

Table 7.9 Views about conflict between the Scots and the English, 1979–1999

Percentage saying 'very' or 'fairly' serious conflict	1979	1992	1999
	15	30	43
Sample size (=100%)	654	957	1,482

Question: 'How serious would you say conflict between the Scots and the English is?'
Sources: Scottish Election Surveys of 1979 and 1992 and Scottish Parliamentary Election Survey 1999

Further analysis, however, indicates that the sense of heightened

conflict is actually greater among 'Scots' than among those who consider themselves 'British', 46 per cent to 39 per cent, a feature confirmed by the fact that, on the 'Moreno' question, it is those at the
Scottish end of the scale who think that conflict between Scotland and
England is serious. Similarly, there are social class differences in perceptions of conflict, but not in the way one might expect. Those in
manual jobs, for example, are in fact more likely to see conflict as
very or fairly serious than the salariat (52 per cent to 32 per cent),
and those who define themselves as working class rather than
middle class do the same (47 per cent to 34 per cent). There is little
evidence, then, that either British identifiers or the middle class think
Scottish–English conflict is serious. Given that English incomers are
more likely to be in middle-class jobs (Dickson 1994), it is hard to
sustain the view that they see themselves as an oppressed minority in
Scotland, for, if anything, it is working-class, Scottish identifiers who
believe that conflict is serious. In fact, the proportion seeing very
or fairly serious conflict is 43 per cent among people not born in
Scotland, and 42 per cent among people born in Scotland, suggesting that place of birth makes very little difference. While we cannot
make direct inferences about the actual state of relations between
Scots-born and English-born people in Scotland, such a finding does
suggest that incomers from England, who account for around 7 per
cent of the Scottish population, do not express a heightened sense of
conflict.

How, then, are we to explain this belief among Scots identifiers
that conflict has grown? One likely explanation is that such a question
is simply measuring a growing awareness and salience of national
differences between Scotland and England, rather than evidence of
actual conflict. In other words, the media possibly have a key role in
amplifying instances of Scottish-English conflict.

WHO IS A SCOT?

The discussion about nationality begs the question about the criteria
for Scottishness. We can find historically different versions of being
Scottish, such that the identity nexus of Union, Empire and
Protestantism provided the pillars on which nineteenth-century
Scottishness was erected (McCrone 1992). Plainly, in a post-imperial
and secular age, and one in which the Union is being re-negotiated

117

in a quite radical way, we cannot assume that the old underpinnings survive. One of the interesting effects of home rule is likely to be that it highlights different ways of being 'Scottish'. For example, living in Scotland conveys the right to vote in parliamentary elections denied to those of Scottish birth living in England. To test different criteria, the 1999 survey asked: 'Say that Scotland did become independent, which of the following kinds of people do you think should be entitled to a Scottish passport?'. This focus on citizenship has the merit of allowing us to compare how restrictive or otherwise people think it should be. In methodological terms it proved to be a simple way of asking how respondents connected the three criteria of birth, residence and descent. The results were as in Table 7.10.

Table 7.10 Views on who should be a Scottish citizen

Category of person	Percentage agreeing such a person should be a Scottish citizen
Born in Scotland and currently living in Scotland	97
Born in Scotland but not currently living in Scotland	79
Not born in Scotland but currently living in Scotland	52
Not born in Scotland, not living in Scotland, but with at least one parent born in Scotland	34
Not born in Scotland, not living in Scotland, but with at least one grandparent born in Scotland	16
Sample size (=100%)	1,482

Question: 'Say that Scotland did become independent, which of the following kinds of people do you think should be entitled to a Scottish passport?'
Source: Scottish Parliamentary Election Survey 1999

Undoubtedly, being born in Scotland – whether or not one lives in Scotland – is taken as the main criterion for being a Scottish citizen, in the event of Scottish independence. While birth is undoubtedly the main criterion for citizenship, it is interesting that just over half are prepared to accept residence over birth, a definition at the more liberal end of the spectrum of citizenship criteria in the new Europe, where barriers to non-Europeans entering the European Union have become much higher (Anderson 2000). Descent, either in terms of parents' or grandparents' origins, is the least important criterion.

Factor analysis indicates that birth, residence and descent are three discrete dimensions, operating relatively independently of each other.

What is more, views about these criteria seem not to be affected by respondents' own sense of identity. The proportion attaching importance to 'born but not live' is 76 per cent among the 'British', and 79 per cent among 'Scots'; while the proportions for 'not born but live' are 58 per cent and 50 per cent respectively. Thus, it seems that people's own identity does not strongly influence their views about other people's identity, possibly because people, in classical liberal fashion, see identity as a private matter. It remains to be seen whether, in the context of a Scottish parliament, any or all of these criteria become politicised, fundamental as these are in defining inclusion and exclusion. Whatever the future holds, all we can say at this stage in Scotland's political history is that issues of national identity are not particularly divisive.

CONCLUSION

The picture which emerges in this chapter is a complex one. It confirms that people in Scotland define themselves first and foremost as Scots, but not at the expense of being British. Hence, our results are in line with surveys since the late 1980s which have shown consistent findings in so far as people locate themselves at the Scottish rather than the British end of the spectrum by a factor of at least six to one (Bond 2000). These are, however, relatively early days in the measurement of national identity, especially by means of surveys. Using the 'Moreno' question with its 5-point scale, or forced national identity (Scottish or British), does not elicit the meanings people give to these categories. The Moreno measure has a robustness to it, for it correlates well and consistently with social variables such as social class, age, gender and educational achievement. The key to Moreno is that people in Scotland, as in Wales, seem to grasp what the question is getting at, namely, the balance between national (Scottish) identity and state (British) identity. In England, there is a tendency towards the middle of the spectrum, equally English and British, but this may simply be a function of greater confusion between the terms (Brown *et al.* 1999). As Anthony Barnett commented, 'the English . . . are more often baffled when asked how they relate their Englishness and Britishness to each other. They often fail to understand how they can be contrasted at all' (1997: 293).

While Scottishness is much stronger north of the border than comparable national identities in other parts of the UK, it has a pervasive effect, colouring virtually all aspects of social and political life. That is why it does not 'explain' support for a parliament in and of itself, for even those who choose to highlight their Britishness are by no means opposed to home rule. At the beginning of this chapter, we raised the possibility of two competing 'effects': the ratchet effect, where one might expect an enhancing of Scottishness in the context of the new politics; and, on the other hand, a dampening effect, where there is less political need to forefront nationality in a more sympathetic political environment, and hence a diminishing of Scottishness. Which is supported by data in this study? On the one hand, there is some evidence of a slipping back from the high point of Scottishness at the time of the 1997 referendum, and, as other chapters in this book show, a less optimistic or more realistic assessment of what such a parliament can achieve. On the other hand, the overall effect is that there has not been a falling back in levels of Scottishness, such that people say they are equally Scottish and British. In any case, our analysis of the panel study (Table 7.2) suggests that identity is rather more fluid than crude political slogans about being Scottish or being British would warrant. People shift in their identification, and so home rule might dampen Scottishness under some circumstances but augment it on other occasions. Whether or not the new parliament has acted as a ratchet, or whether there has been a growing sense of Scottishness regardless of constitutional change, will only become apparent as the new politics of Scotland unfold. This politics is taking place around a new constitutional divide, home rule versus independence, which has superseded the previous debate about whether there should be any constitutional change at all. The Scottish Parliament is likely to become the embodiment of political identity, and, as such, become an important emblem of 'being Scottish'. We would do well to remember that national identity is not so much a matter of sentiment, as of social and political practice.

8

THE POLITICS OF
SOCIAL WELFARE

------·······Λ₽ΛΛΛΛ------

INTRODUCTION

In this chapter and the next, we look at the policy demands that
might be made on the new Scottish Parliament, how far these
demands are different from England, and whether they are pushing
the party competiton in different directions in Scotland. This chapter
deals with general debates about the future of the welfare state in
Scotland; Chapter 9 deals with specific questions about education.

On welfare, we look at three questions. The first is a re-examination
of the belief that Scotland is more left-wing than England. That claim
has been assessed several times in the last decade, with the conclusion
usually being that Scotland is somewhat more left-wing, but not as
strongly different as its different voting behaviour would suggest
(Brown *et al.* 1998; Brown *et al.* 1999; Curtice 1988, 1996). Thus the
finding has generally been that Scotland tends to be more in favour
of state action to overcome inequalities of wealth, and more supportive of state provision in key parts of the welfare state such as
health and education, but that the striking feature of the 1980s and
early 1990s was in fact that England remained left of centre even
while it was electing the governments of Margaret Thatcher and
John Major. The question now is whether that pattern showed any

sign of changing around the time of the first elections to the Scottish Parliament. The reason for asking the question again is that, in at least one high-profile respect, the SNP tried to push the debate to the left in 1999, when they claimed that Scots would be more willing than people in England to vote for a party that offered to use higher taxes to pay for better public services.

The second debate is about Scotland's position on the more general matter of whether and how the welfare state needs to be renewed. On the one hand, in the words of Esping-Andersen (1996: 27), in many developed countries there is widespread popular support for the view that 'as mechanisms for social integration, the eradication of class differences, and nation-building, the advanced welfare states have been hugely successful'. On the other hand, as Pierson (1991: 195) puts it, 'the types of welfare state which we will inhabit . . . seem liable to change under the impact of a range of economic, social, political and ecological pressures'. There will be more variety of welfare forms. Benefits will become more selective, in some places public services will become minimal, in the sense of providing only for those who cannot pay for their own services, and there will be a shift away from tax-based towards contributory means of paying for it all (ibid.: 185). The particular connection with constitutional reform is that the governance of the welfare state may become more decentralised, which would have potentially significant implications for universal standards (Pierson 1991: 198–200).

The most thorough empirical examination of popular views on these matters across Britain as a whole has been carried out by Hills and Lelkes (1999), who conclude that 'there is a striking resemblance between many of the new Labour government's initial measures on social security and the electorate's overall preferences' (21) – notably a popular preference for some wealth redistribution, but also for a more efficient targeting of benefits, and a common view that the benefit system 'undermines independence and the will to work' (20). Hills and Lelkes used the 1998 British Social Attitudes Survey (and some of its predecessors), which had no special over-sampling of people in Scotland, and so could not give a detailed picture of any distinctive views there. From the Scottish Parliamentary Election Survey we do not have access to the full range of detailed questions about benefit levels that Hills and Lelkes used, but we do have a variety of measures that test more general attitudes to the welfare state, and so we can go some way to deciding whether the conclusions reached by Hills and Lelkes are applicable to Scotland.

The third debate is then how Scottish attitudes to the welfare state and to New Labour's policies on it relate to political arguments in and around the Scottish Parliament, and to views about the future evolution of the powers of the Parliament. At present, the Parliament has very strong powers over those parts of the welfare state that provide services – health, education, housing, social work. It has almost no powers over benefits or taxation. Do Scottish views about the welfare state provide any clues about how Scots would like to see the powers of the Parliament evolving? Part of the answer to that will be in the party-political conflicts in Scotland. In England, there is no electorally viable party that is significantly to the left of New Labour, and so people who find the government's approach to welfare insufficiently redistributive or insufficiently generous have few options open to them. In Scotland, the situation is more complex. At least rhetorically, the SNP is to the left of Labour on welfare issues, and – partly because of the proportional electoral system – the Scottish Socialist Party offers a viable option that is unambiguously in favour of old styles of socialism. Does this more competitive political environment in Scotland make the politics of welfare more difficult for Labour than in England? And what about people to the right of Labour in Scotland? They would seem to have only one viable option, the Tories, who remain moribund, as we have seen in Chapters 3, 4 and 5.

So the chapter provides Scottish evidence on two fundamental questions about the future of the welfare state that have resonance in many countries. Is there a popular basis for renewing the welfare state? And can constitutional reform help or impede in that renewal – for example, help it by decentralising provision, or impede it by entrenching what might be seen as a rather conservative attachment to the values of Old Labour?

The chapter is in three sections. The first two debates – is Scotland different, and are New Labour policies popular? – are dealt with in the first section, by comparing Scottish and English views on a range of questions about the welfare state. We postpone looking at educational issues until Chapter 9, because we have the data to look at these in greater depth. The second section examines the ways in which views about public welfare impinge on voting, and in particular looks at whether people in Scotland who favour a strong welfare state are more likely to have abandoned the Labour Party between 1997 and 1999 than similar people in England. The last section considers whether people are likely to draw from these debates any long-term implications for the powers of the Scottish Parliament.

VIEWS OF THE WELFARE STATE

Table 8.1 shows Scottish and English attitudes to the need for public welfare, and Table 8.2 shows attitudes to the role of government in providing welfare. The first point to take from the tables is the broad similarity of views in the two countries: it seems that the new context of the Scottish Parliamentary election, and two years of a UK Labour government, had not affected that long-standing conclusion. Thus, in both places, Table 8.1 shows substantial majorities believing that income inequality is too high, that ordinary people do not get a fair share of wealth, that power is unequally shared ('one law for the rich and one for the poor'), and that people fail to claim benefits to which they are entitled. From Table 8.2, we see also that large majorities believe that the government is responsible for dealing with some of the central social problems that have always been the

**Table 8.1 Views on need for public welfare,
Scotland and England**

Percentages agreeing	Scotland	England
Income inequality in Britain is too high	87	83
Ordinary people get their fair share of nation's wealth	17	14
There is one law for the rich and one for the poor	67	62
Redistribute income and wealth	61	36
Large numbers of people who are eligible for benefits fail to claim them	83	85
Benefits for unemployed people are too low and cause hardship	38	33
Benefits for unemployed people are too high and discourage them from finding jobs	35	46
Sample size (=100%)	1,482	2,718

Sources: Scottish Parliamentary Election Survey 1999; British Social Attitudes Survey 1999

124

preoccupation of the welfare state – the effects of ill-health, retire-ment, disability, unemployment and old age. There is fairly clear support for more public spending to cope with these matters, even if that meant taxes rising (note that the question about more gov-ernment spending on disabled people etc. reminded respondents that taxes may have to rise to allow that).

Table 8.2 Views on government responsibility for and spending on public welfare, Scotland and England

Percentages agreeing	Scotland	England
The government is mainly responsible for:		
health care	87	85
maintaining retired people	64	59
maintaining disabled people	87	84
maintaining unemployed people	88	88
residential care of elderly people	89	84
Government should increase taxes and spend		
more on health, education and social benefits	56	58
More government spending on:*		
disabled people	70	62
parents on low income	72	70
retired people	70	71
carers for sick or elderly	82	84
Sample size (=100%)	1,482	2,718

*Respondents were reminded that increased spending might lead to higher taxes
Sources: Scottish Parliamentary Election Survey 1999; British Social Attitudes Survey 1999

Also in line with past findings is the more nuanced point that Scottish views tend to be to the left of English views on most of these measures, but usually by only a few percentage points. For example (Table 8.2), whereas in England 59 per cent of people believe that the government is mainly responsible for ensuring that retired people have a reasonable standard of living, in Scotland the proportion is 64 per cent. There is a rather larger gap in attitudes to unemployed people (Table 8.1): only 35 per cent of Scots believe that benefits are too high, in contrast to 46 per cent of people in England, although it should be noted that Hills and Lelkes report that, when informed about the actual levels of these benefits, a large majority of their British sample said that they were too low to live on (Hills and Lelkes 1999: 11–12). There is a very large gap on the general question about redistributing income and wealth (61 per cent support in Scotland, 36 per cent in England). But the overall picture is of Scotland's being slightly to the left of England.

The large difference on redistribution, while there is only a small difference on perceptions of inequality (Table 8.1), may reveal that the language in which these debates are conducted is different in Scotland and England: 'redistribution' remains in the respectable political lexicon in Scotland, so that what Hills and Lelkes call 'redistribution by stealth' may be more necessary in England than in Scotland. That word is the main apparent difference in the two questions here: the first asked whether 'income and wealth should be redistributed towards ordinary working people' and the second asked for views about 'the gap between those with high incomes and those with low incomes'. It may also be relevant that the second prefaced the question by asking people to think about 'income levels generally in Britain today'; perhaps the absence of a reference to Britain in the question about redistribution allowed people to think in terms of a specifically Scottish debate. This possibility that it is the politics and national context of the issue which matters is relevant to our later discussion of the politics of welfare in the two countries.

These patterns all seem to have been evolving for some time, but not in any clear direction, as is shown in Table 8.3, which looks at three of the measures in successive election surveys going back to 1992 and (for redistribution) to 1979. Scotland seems to have maintained a level of support for redistribution that has not changed much since the 1970s, while English support has declined. On the other hand, at least since 1992, England has converged towards Scotland in perceiving that wealth and power are not fairly distributed. It may be that the processes leading to the advent of a Labour government in 1997 induced a more common British view of inequalities in society, even while Scots retained a stronger commitment than people in England to doing something about it. We return to this point about changes over time in the next section, when we examine how changed attitudes relate to changing propensities to vote for the Labour Party.

Scotland and England appear to be quite similar also in their views about the effects of the welfare state on people's behaviour. As Hills

Table 8.3 Views on welfare Scotland and England, 1979–1999

	Scotland		England	
	Percentage agreeing	*Sample size (=100%)*	*Percentage agreeing*	*Sample size (=100%)*
Redistribute income and wealth				
1979	58	729	52	1,641
1992	61	957	47	2,428
1997	69	882	59	2,551
1999	61	1,482	36	2,718
Ordinary people get their fair share of nation's wealth				
1992	17	957	24	2,428
1997	12	882	16	2,551
1999	17	1,482	14	2,718
There is one law for the rich and one for the poor				
1992	70	957	56	2,428
1997	80	882	71	2,551
1999	67	1,482	62	2,718

Sources: Scottish and British Election Surveys 1979; Scottish and British Election Surveys 1992; Scottish and British Election Surveys 1997; Scottish Parliamentary Election Survey 1999; British Social Attitudes Survey 1999

and Lelkes (1999: 20) note, there is 'a widespread public concern about the dangers of undermining independence and the will to work through too high benefits'. Tables 8.4 and 8.5 show some of the details. Note that Table 8.4 has to be treated with some caution: these questions about the effects of welfare were not asked in the Scottish Parliamentary Election Survey, and so in order to gain an adequate Scottish sample size, two years (1998 and 1999) of the British Social Attitudes Survey have been combined. Thus any change between 1998 and 1999 has been obscured, and even then the Scottish sample size is only moderately large (549). As in England, substantial minorities in Scotland believe that the welfare state makes people less willing to look after themselves and less willing to help each other (Table 8.4). In Scotland and in England, there is much less enthusiasm for public spending on unemployed people and on lone

parents than on other potential recipients such as disabled people
(Table 8.5 compared to Table 8.2), and almost everyone in both
countries believes that many welfare recipients claim benefits to
which they are not entitled (Table 8.5).

**Table 8.4 Views on effects of welfare state,
Scotland and England**

Percentages agreeing	Scotland	England
Unemployed could find job if wanted	44	57
Welfare state makes people less willing to look after themselves	47	48
Reducing welfare would make people stand on own two feet	30	40
Welfare state stops people helping each other	35	34
Social security recipients made to feel like second–class citizens	39	43
Sample sizes (=100%)	549	5,413

Source: British Social Attitudes Surveys 1998 and 1999 combined

**Table 8.5 Views on effects of welfare state,
Scotland and England**

Percentages agreeing	Scotland	England
Large numbers of people falsely claim benefits	90	87
More government spending on:		
unemployed	26	24
lone parents	35	33
Sample sizes (=100%)	1,482	2,718

Sources: Scottish Parliamentary Election Survey 1999; British Social Attitudes Survey 1999

Again, Scottish views are somewhat less harsh than those in England.
Whereas a majority (57 per cent) in England believe that unemployed
people could find a job if they wanted to, only 44 per cent of Scots
take that view (Table 8.4), although it should be noted that the
question asked about jobs 'around here', and so the answers could
be coloured by any persisting belief that unemployment is higher
in Scotland than in England (even though it isn't). Withdrawing

welfare is a less popular means of promoting personal independence in Scotland (30 per cent support) than in England (40 per cent). And the demeaning effects of social security are probably less widely perceived in Scotland (39 per cent) than in England (43 per cent).

There is some regional variation in England. On the questions where there are small differences between Scotland and England, Scotland seems to be at the end of a north–south gradient that starts north of the English Midlands. For example, the proportion believing that government is responsible for ensuring that retired people have an adequate income was 56 per cent in southern England, 60 per cent in the Midlands, 62 per cent in northern England, and (from Table 8.2) 64 per cent in Scotland. Likewise, the proportion believing that benefits for unemployed people are too high was 46 per cent in southern England, 50 per cent in the Midlands, 43 per cent in northern England and 35 per cent in Scotland. The proportion believing that reducing welfare would make people stand on their own two feet was 41 per cent in southern England, 46 per cent in the Midlands, 38 per cent in northern England and (from Table 8.4) 30 per cent in Scotland. The one exception is, again, redistribution of wealth. The English proportions in favour were 36 per cent in the south, 34 per cent in the Midlands, and 39 per cent in the North, all far below the Scottish proportion of 61 per cent (Table 8.1).

So Scotland seems to be somewhat more supportive of the welfare state than England, but not decisively more so. Scotland shares with England a perception that society is unequal, and a belief that the state should use taxes to help put that right. We will examine in Chapter 9 whether the same can be said of national differences in views of a public education system (Tables 8.1–8.3). The two countries also agree, however, that old ways of achieving a fairer society have regrettable side effects, such as discouraging independence and the will to work. The very marked Scottish difference in views about redistribution (Table 8.1) suggests, nevertheless, that these views are quite consistent with a preference for radical political action of some sort.

We can now answer one of our initial questions. The advent of the Scottish Parliament generally has not in itself widened the policy divide between Scotland and England, and so there should be no reason, in principle, for frustration in Scotland at the parliament's lack of powers over key aspects of welfare policy – such as social security and taxation. But whether people believe that Westminster ought to be in charge of these activities, despite this, cannot be decided by this coincidence of views: at least as important is how these views relate to party competitition north and south of the border. Views about welfare do not show that there is a distinctive Scottish political culture, but the mere presence of the Scottish Parliament may allow these views to be articulated in ways that are not available in England.

THE WELFARE STATE AND VOTING

The politics of the welfare state do not depend only on attitudes. In a parliamentary democracy, the really important shaping influence is how these attitudes relate to partisan preference – what parties people choose to represent their attitudes. Now that Scotland has its own parliament, the interaction between popular views and popular preferences among parties matters more than in the unreformed Union. For Scottish social policy to evolve in the same direction as social policy in England would require not only that social attitudes were broadly the same in the two countries, but also that they were picked up by the parties in broadly the same way, and that the resulting votes were translated into seats in the same way.

The obvious distinguishing feature of Scottish party politics that complicates the relationship between popular attitudes and policy is the presence of the SNP, a party broadly of the left that is able to challenge Labour for dominance of Scottish politics. That electoral battle has been analysed in detail in earlier chapters; the point here is to see how it relates to views about social welfare. Although the SNP is the main distinctive feature of the Scottish party system, it is not the only one, especially now that the electoral system for the Scottish Parliament is so different from that for the UK Parliament. Because of their presence in the Scottish Parliament, the Scottish Socialist Party and the Greens make an impact on public debate in Scotland that is greater than anything made by similar parties in England. Moreover, because these three parties are all on the left in their policies, the position of the other parties cannot but be affected too. Thus, whereas in England the Liberal Democrats are evolving as the only viable left-of-centre alternative to Labour, in Scotland they are faced with several rivals in that role. Because the Liberal Democrats are also a unionist party, they may be able to attract right-of-centre Tory votes more readily than in England.

These points about party policies on social welfare do seem to be reflected in the social attitudes of their supporters. Table 8.6 looks at the differences by party identification in three of the attitudes to the welfare state which we have been examining: views about income inequality, redistribution of income and wealth, and the level of benefits for the unemployed. Party identification is the response to the question 'generally speaking, do you think of yourself as . . .?'. The first point to note is that, in Scotland, supporters of the Labour Party and of the SNP are very similar in their views, supporters of the Conservatives are to the right of them, and those of the Liberal Democrats are in between. This pattern of views about social policy is not surprising when we consider the analysis in Chapter 4 of the social values held by supporters of the parties: people seem to translate left-of-centre values (Table 4.7) quite reliably into left-of-centre positions on policy (Table 8.6).

In England, by contrast, Liberal Democrat supporters are much closer to supporters of the Labour party than to supporters of the Conservatives. So the table seems to confirm the partisan identities that could be inferred from party differences in policy. In Scotland, the main left-of-centre rival to Labour is the SNP, whereas in England it is the Liberal Democrats. As a result, the Scottish Liberal Democrats have proportionately more right-of-centre supporters than do the Liberal Democrats in England.

However, the difficulty of drawing inferences such as these from one survey in isolation is that it tells us nothing about how people move among parties, and so is not very revealing about the political dynamics of social welfare. What we really need to know, for example, is whether people move directly from Labour to the SNP in response to UK or Scottish government policy. That would be a better test of any claim that the politics of social welfare in Scotland is different from that in England. We do have a data source that can track such changes: the British Election Panel Study. This takes the people who were in the British and Scottish Election Surveys of 1997, and re-interviews them at annual intervals. Thus we can investigate how individuals changed their views or their party support between 1997 and 1999. The disadvantage of doing this is that sample numbers are smaller than in the 1999 Scottish Parliamentary Election Survey,

**Table 8.6 Views on welfare by party identification,
Scotland and England**

Percentages agreeing	Scotland				England		
	Con	Lab	Lib Dem	SNP	Con	Lab	Lib Dem
Income inequality in Britain too high	80	90	86	86	72	88	90
Redistribute income and wealth	36	69	58	64	22	44	42
Benefits for unemployed people are too low and cause hardship	22	45	32	40	24	37	37
Sample sizes (=100%)	231	625	166	290	722	1,148	280

Party identified with is the response to the question 'generally speaking, do you think
of yourself as . . .?'.
Sources: Scottish Parliamentary Election Survey 1999; British Social Attitudes Survey 1999

partly because the 1997 Scottish survey was smaller in the first place
(882 people), and partly because not everyone who was interviewed
in 1997 agreed to be re-interviewed in 1998 and 1999 (only about
seven in ten did so: see Appendix). Nevertheless, the trends do give
some indication of how opinion is moving. The main attrition is
among people who did not vote in 1997, who are not considered in
this analysis.

The measures available from the Panel Study are not so detailed
as we have been examining so far – for example, specific questions
about redistribution, inequality or the effects of welfare benefits on
incentives to work. Instead, respondents were asked for their views
on two broad propositions concerning taxation, spending and
income redistribution, and asked for their responses on a 11-point
scale, augmented by two extra points for people to the left of the
left-most point as offered to respondents, and people to the right of
the right-most. The two propositions are shown in Table 8.7 and the
mean replies are shown for Scotland and England in 1997, 1998 and
1999. For the mean responses, the points on the augmented scale

were numbered 0–12, low values being left-wing and high values being right-wing.

**Table 8.7 Views on need for public welfare,
Scotland and England, 1997–1999**

	Scotland		England	
	Means on scales (low = left wing)	Standard Error	Means on scales (low = left wing)	Standard Error
Government should put up taxes a lot and spend much more on health and social services				
1997	3.49	0.14	3.74	0.05
1998	4.04	0.17	4.05	0.05
1999	3.75	0.16	3.99	0.05
Government should make much greater effort to make people's incomes more equal				
1997	3.62	0.18	4.37	0.07
1998	4.03	0.20	4.82	0.07
1999	4.09	0.20	5.08	0.08

Sources: British Election Panel Study 1997, 1998 and 1999

The first point to note is that, at almost all time points and for each question, Scotland is to the left of England: for example, in 1999, the mean response on redistributing income was 4.09 in Scotland and 5.08 in England. In the year following the election of the 1997 Labour government, people in Scotland and England moved to the right on these questions, but then in 1999 an interesting divergence opened up. On government spending, Scotland moved left again (although not as far back as it had been in 1997), whereas England broadly remained at the same position as in 1998. On redistribution, England moved further right than in 1998, while Scotland remained roughly at the 1998 position. The net effect was that, on attitudes to government spending in 1999, Scotland was as far to the left of England as it had been in 1997, while on attitudes to income redistribution in 1999, Scotland was more to the left of England than it had been in 1997. These broad patterns are consistent with the more detailed comparisons shown in Table 8.1, confirming that the responses to the scale questions in the Panel Study are picking up the same kinds of patterns as were obtained from the Scottish Parliamentary Election Survey and the British Social Attitudes Survey in 1999.

Remembering still that the Panel Study is tracking the views of the same group of people from 1997 to 1999, these preliminary impressions from Table 8.7 raise questions about the shifting relationship between people's views about public welfare and their perceptions of the Labour government's policies (measured by a similarly phrased survey question). The net result is shown in Table 8.8, which summarises where people stood ideologically in relation to their perception of Labour in 1997 and 1999. In both Scotland and England, there was a rise from about one-third to just over four out of ten people seeing themselves as being to the left of Labour in this sense on the spending scale, with corresponding drops in

Table 8.8 Ideological position in relation to Labour on need for public welfare, Scotland and England, 1997–1999

	Scotland		England	
	1997	*1999*	*1997*	*1999*
Government should put up taxes a lot and spend much more on health and social services				
to left of Labour	32	45	32	42
same as Labour	37	26	34	30
to right of Labour	31	28	34	28
Government should make much greater efforts to make people's incomes more equal				
to left of Labour	35	45	28	34
same as Labour	36	24	31	22
to right of Labour	30	30	41	45
Sample sizes (=100%)	626	626	1,813	1,813

Sources: British Election Panel Study 1997 and 1999

the proportions sharing a position with Labour or placing themselves to the right of Labour. On the redistribution scale, the pattern was similar in Scotland, but in England there was a consistently
lower left-wing proportion: 28 per cent in 1997 and 34 per cent in
1999.

What is more, in Scotland, this net shift to the left of Labour was
occurring at the same time as a sharp net shift in the perception of
the SNP in relation to Labour, as Table 8.9 shows. In 1997, under a
quarter of voters saw the SNP as being to the left of Labour, but by
1999 this had risen to four out of ten on taxes and spending, and
one third on inequality. In neither Scotland nor England was there
much movement in the perception of the other main parties in
relation to Labour. For example, on taxes and spending, in 1997 and
in 1999, and in both Scotland and England, just under one-third
placed the Liberal Democrats to the left of Labour, and just over
one-third placed them in the same position as Labour.

**Table 8.9 Perception of SNP's ideological position in relation
to Labour, 1997–1999**

Percentage	1997	1999
Government should put up taxes a lot and spend much more on health and social services		
SNP to left of Labour	23	40
SNP same as Labour	38	30
SNP to right of Labour	39	31
Government should make much greater efforts to make people's incomes more equal		
SNP to left of Labour	19	32
SNP same as Labour	37	33
SNP to right of Labour	44	35
Sample sizes (=100%)	626	626

Sources: British Election Panel Study 1997 and 1999

The political question is now how these different groups of people
behaved. Did the fact of having embarked on a different ideological

trajectory from Labour induce people to abandon Labour voting, and, in Scotland, did a perception that the SNP is to the left of Labour incline left-wing people to move towards that party? Because there was no national election in England in 1999, we measure voting intentions there by how people said they would have voted in a general election if one had taken place (a measure that we also used in Chapter 3). For Scotland, we use the vote which people reported in the regional element of the election for the Scottish Parliament. We have chosen the regional vote because it was that part of the election in which people showed the strongest propensity to experiment, although in fact the conclusions reached are broadly the same if the constituency element is used. So the main question we are testing now is whether the new context of the Scottish Parliament elections encouraged electoral experimentation by people who were to the left of Labour or who saw Labour drifting rightwards. If we do find this, then we have some evidence that the new Scottish political situation has started to bring into being a new politics of welfare.

We concentrate the discussion on what happened to people who voted Labour in the 1997 general election. That is for three reasons. One is that, because Labour dominates Scottish politics (and has done so since the 1970s), the most immediately relevant changes in voting behaviour take the form of movement away from that party. The second reason is that Labour is the original party of the welfare state, and part of the claim of New Labour is that only it can be trusted to modernise the welfare state in a manner that is consistent with its founding principles; thus movement away from Labour would put that claim about trust to the test. The third reason for concentrating on Labour is simply that it has power: it forms the government in Westminster, and leads the coalition in Scotland. So defections from Labour are politically interesting because ultimately they may mean a change of government in one or both of these places.

A simple breakdown of the vote in 1997 and 1999, in Scotland and England, according to voters' ideological position in relation to Labour, suggests that Labour's problem in Scotland is not just that more voters are now to their left than before. In England, Labour's share of each ideological group was much the same in 1999 as in 1997, or higher: on taxes and spending, for example, they had the support of 48 per cent of the group to their left, 59 per cent of the group who were in the same position as them, and 36 per cent of the group to their right, and the gap between 48 per cent and 59 per cent is not large enough to cause the greater size of the left-wing group in 1999, in itself, to have a big impact on Labour support. The pattern for inequality was similar, except that Labour actually picked up a greater share of the group to their right in 1999 than in 1997: 40 per cent compared with 29 per cent. In Scotland, by contrast, Labour in 1997 lost particularly heavily among both people to their left and people to their right. On taxes, they got 50 per cent of the left-wing group in 1997, but only 32 per cent in 1999; they got 43 per cent of the right-wing group in 1997, and 29 per cent in 1999. Only their share of the group which was close to the party ideologically was only slighltly down, from 62 per cent to 56 per cent. The patterns of Labour loss were similar in terms of views about inequality.

That analysis was in terms of entire ideological groups, regardless of how they had previously voted. But what happened to 1997 Labour voters? A detailed analysis of their movements is given in Table 8.10. It shows how 1997 Labour voters voted in 1999 (or, in England, said they would have voted in a general election), according to their ideological position in relation to their perception of Labour's ideological position. In England, the vast majority of 1997 Labour voters was still supporting Labour two years later, regardless of where they stood ideologically in relation to Labour. For example, on the government spending scale, 80 per cent of 1997 Labour voters who were to the left of Labour in 1999 still supported Labour. The proportion for 1997 Labour voters who were to the right of Labour by 1999 was almost the same: 78 per cent. In Scotland, by contrast, Labour seems to have lost people to both its left and its right. On the spending scale, 40 per cent of 1997 Labour voters on the left of Labour abandoned Labour. Likewise, 41 per cent of those to the right of Labour defected. The only group which seems to have remained as loyal to Labour as in England were those who shared Labour's ideological position: for example, on government spending, 81 per cent of such people remained loyal. The problem for Labour is that this group is small: from Table 8.8, we see that it makes up just a quarter of the whole electorate, although it did make up around one-third of 1997 Labour voters in both Scotland and England.

Table 8.10 1999 vote among 1997 Labour voters, by ideological position in relation to Labour, Scotland and England

Percentage Labour in 1999*	Scotland		England	
Ideological position in relation to Labour in 1999:	%	Sample size (=100%)	%	Sample size (=100%)
Government should put up taxes a lot and spend much more on health and social services				
to left of Labour	60	107	80	273
same as Labour	81	82	87	234
to right of Labour	59	58	78	139
Government should make much greater efforts to make people's incomes more equal				
to left of Labour	55	122	75	265
same as Labour	84	71	89	128
to right of Labour	67	56	84	437

*Scotland: regional vote in Scottish Parliament elections; England: vote in a hypothetical general election held at the time of the survey; non-voters have been excluded
Sources: British Election Panel Study 1997 and 1999

Where did these ex-Labour people go in Scotland? Of those to the left of Labour, around one-half of defectors went to the SNP and around one in five went to the SSP or the Greens. To the right of Labour, about one in ten went to each of the SNP, the Liberal Democrats and the Greens. The Conservatives benefited from almost none of this in Scotland: among 1997 Labour voters who in 1999 were to the right of Labour on government spending, just one in twenty defectors went to the Tories. Among those to the right on redistribution, one in six went to the Tories. In England, where defections from Labour were in any case fewer, most of those to the right of Labour went to the Tories. Of those to the right of Labour on government spending, over one-half of defectors went to the Tories. Of the analogous group on redistribution, two-thirds of defectors went to that party.

Adding to Labour's problems with welfare issues in Scotland is that they do not compensate for their losses with gains from people who voted for other parties in 1997. Fifteen per cent or fewer of such people voted Labour on the regional lists in 1999, regardless of where they placed themselves or Labour ideologically. In England, by contrast, Labour attracted around one-fifth of people who did not support the party in 1997.

So the electoral politics of welfare in Scotland are being expressed in new ways. As the rhetoric of the party battles would suggest, it is partly that – unlike in England – there are two or three parties to the left of Labour who can capture people who are themselves to the left of Labour. The main gainers in this movement are the SNP and the Scottish Socialist Party. But Labour also loses sizeable minorities of its supporters who are to the right of Labour. The main benefi-ciaries are again the SNP (although to a lesser extent than among left-wingers), the Greens and the Liberal Democrats. These move-ments to the right of Labour in Scotland are not happening in England either.

None of this rightwards movement seems to correspond to differ-ences in the parties' ideological positions, since none of these parties is ostensibly to the right of Labour. Nevertheless, further analysis of voters' perceptions of the SNP suggests that the movement towards that party may be partly due to varying perceptions of the ideological relationship between it and Labour, depending on the voter's own relationship to Labour. People who were themselves to the left of Labour tended to perceive the SNP as being to the left of Labour: 56 per cent of such people did so on the tax question, as did 48 per cent (the largest group) on the inequality question. That would correspond with how the SNP wants to present itself. But, rather awkwardly for the SNP's current public position, voters with different relationships to Labour's ideology saw the SNP as either identical to or to the right of Labour. Thus, among people who shared Labour's ideological position, the largest groups – 43 per cent on tax and 49 per cent on inequality – perceived the SNP as also sharing Labour's ideology. And, among people who were to the right of Labour, again the largest groups – 45 per cent on tax and 52 per cent on inequality – saw the SNP as being to the right of Labour. Whether Labour (or SNP left-wingers) like it or not, the SNP does seem to be able to be all things to all people.

All of this movement in Scotland is taking place even though opinion on government spending and redistribution of income has moved in much the same direction as in England, and even though perceptions of Labour's positions on these matters have also moved similarly in the two countries. The explanations seem to be a mixture of a more plural party system in Scotland and the proportional electoral system, in the new Scottish context of the first election to the parliament and therefore at a self-conscious distance from the UK Labour government in London. Whatever the explanation, the main point to take from this section is that to understand the politics of welfare we have to look beyond a mere description of people's views on aspects of inequality and the welfare state; these views do place Scotland to the left of England, but not by much. A different politics of welfare emerges because similar views interact in different ways with the new voting opportunities created by the new proportional electoral system and the new Parliament, such that people dissenting in various ways from Labour find places to go in Scotland that seem not to be available in England. Since this is a product of the new Scottish governing system, the final question to which we turn in this chapter is how that system itself might be influenced by the politics of welfare.

THE SCOTTISH PARLIAMENT AND THE WELFARE STATE

If it is the new Scottish governing system that is causing the decay of old loyalties around the welfare state, do people in Scotland expect that the Parliament is likely to become the main way in which their own views about welfare can be translated into practice? From the time of the 1997 referendum, there were very high expectations that the Parliament would improve welfare in Scotland, although, as we saw in Chapter 6, these had moderated somewhat by 1999. But there could be two reactions to that greater realism. One would be to come to think of the Parliament as irrelevant to welfare; the other might be to come to believe that only a stronger parliament than was taking over power in 1999 could achieve the ideals that were strong in 1997. We have also seen in Chapter 6 that a majority of people do think that the Parliament ought to become the main focus of Scottish politics, and so it seems unlikely that the first of these views about the Parliament and welfare would be the stronger, but that still leaves questions. Do people who are strong believers in the ideals of the welfare state favour a stronger parliament to a greater extent than those who take a more right-wing position? Both these groups seem to have experimented with their party loyalties in 1999, and so maybe both would be willing to experiment constitutionally as well.

We return here to the 1999 Scottish Parliamentary Election Survey, since this asked about the evolution of the Parliament's powers. (The question on powers was analysed in depth in Chapter 6.) The first point to note is that, on most measures, the more left-wing people were, the more likely they were to favour an increase in powers. One of the clearest instances is on the question about there being one law for the rich and one for the poor. Among those who agreed, 66 per cent wanted more powers. Among those who took an intermediate position, 47 per cent wanted more powers. Among those who disagreed, 41 per cent wanted more powers. A similar although weaker gradient is found for the questions on income inequality, falsely claiming benefits, and the level of benefit for the unemployed. So there does seem to be some reason to believe that people who are favourable to some of the core principles of the welfare state are in favour of an extension of the Parliament's powers, and it would not seem unreasonable to infer that they would link these two: that they would expect a more powerful parliament to be a route to a stronger welfare state in Scotland.

But the patterns are in fact more interesting than that, corresponding to our finding in the previous section that people to the right of Labour were experimenting with the new party system almost as much as people on the left. This is clearest on the question about people getting a fair share of wealth. It is true that the highest proportion wanting more powers for the Parliament (61 per cent) was among those who disagreed that ordinary people get a fair share, but there was also a majority (55 per cent) for more powers among those who took the opposite view. The most sceptical about more powers were actually those who had no clear view about the extent of inequality. There was, likewise, no difference in the proportions wanting more powers between those who thought that lots of people fail to claim benefits to which they are entitled and those who did not think this (each 58 per cent). Indeed, we find that only two groups had a clear majority (around 60 per cent) against increasing the Parliament's powers – the small minorities who disagreed that there is one law for the rich and one for the poor, and who opposed the redistribution of wealth. These were also the only groups who had sizeable support for decreasing the Parliament's powers, and indeed no group – not even these – had a majority for that approach. So, unlike during the long years of Conservative government, the Scottish Parliament is not seen only as a device for defending Scottish social democracy: that was the long-standing hope of advocates of a parliament, and the fear of its mainly right-wing opponents. The parliament has come to be seen as the natural forum for debates about welfare, but people seem no longer to assume that these debates will necessarily lead to certain left-of-centre outcomes.

CONCLUSION

It seems reasonable to conclude, then, that the Scottish Parliament has become the focus of the politics of the welfare state in Scotland. That is broadly not because Scotland is markedly to the left of England, or of the regions of England. On the whole, both countries do fit into the conclusions reached by Hills and Lelkes (1999) – that there is continuing support for redistribution but also a feeling that the old style of welfare state sapped initiative. The distinctive feature of the politics of welfare in Scotland is now that Scottish views are translated into voting behaviour that has a new forum for expression, and a new proportional system for expressing it. People to both the left and the right of Labour are moving away from the party in Scotland, but not in England. The SNP benefits from both types of movement, although more from leftwards than from rightwards defectors. The Scottish Socialists are also becoming a significant destination for Labour defectors moving leftwards, while the Liberal Democrats and the Greens seem to attract those moving to the right.

The occasion for these defections is a combination of the new political institution, the proportional electoral system and two years of a Labour government at Westminster, and so there is a variety of explanations. Nevertheless, the key point is the Scottish Parliament, because voting changes now have the potential to lead to a change of government in Scotland. That almost all groups – regardless of their views on government spending and redistribution – think that the Parliament should have more powers than at present suggests that they all see it as the forum in which the future of the Scottish welfare state should be decided. The politics of welfare and the politics of the Scottish constitution are now inextricably intertwined.

9

EDUCATION AND
CIVIC IDENTITY

INTRODUCTION

Education is worth examining separately from social policy more
generally for at least three reasons. First, it is an area in which the
Scottish Parliament has almost unfettered power: the only aspect of
educational policy where its remit is limited is in the funding of
some aspects of research in higher education. Second, education was
a salient issue in the election campaign in 1999, especially in the
controversy over whether students in higher education should pay
fees. Finally, education has featured strongly in debates about Scottish
identity, as it has in similar debates in many other small nations. The
sheer prominence of education is one reason to expect that there will
be policy divergence between Scotland and England.

Nevertheless, education can indeed be seen as just another important instance of social policy. Along with health, it appears repeatedly
in opinion polls as the main concern of voters in the UK, and the
Scottish Parliamentary Election Survey was no exception: 27 per
cent named it as the first priority for government spending, and 36
per cent as second priority, giving an overall rating of 63 per cent
that was surpassed only by health (79 per cent) and was far ahead of
the nearest rival, housing (17 per cent). That may be because voters

share politicians' common view that a well-educated labour force is a key to national prosperity (Ashton and Green 1996): certainly, all four main parties in the 1999 Scottish elections subscribed to that belief, as they had done for many decades (Paterson 2000b). Voters are also probably well aware of education as a means of personal social mobility – the route by which they, or their children, could acquire better jobs and hence better chances in life. Again, this is common across the developed world (Heath and Clifford 1990). The resulting popular concern with education as a means of realising social justice has ensured that support for equality of opportunity in education became, during the second half of the twentieth century, one of the most deeply entrenched principles of welfare policy (Goldthorpe 1996). Examining details of attitudes to education policy therefore provides depth on one aspect of the general theme of attitudes to the welfare state.

There are, however, more particular reasons to look at attitudes to education in the context of the first elections to the Scottish Parliament. Education has been at the heart of debates about culture and Scottish self-government for over a century. Indeed, it is usually cited as one of the famous three pillars of Scottish identity, along with the legal system and the church – their autonomy guaranteed in various ways by the Treaty of Union in 1707 (Paterson 2000b). When the Union was working well, the old governing class of Scottish education always had a sense of the Scottish national interest in their minds while they were governing, even though, since the mid-twentieth century, they have also tended to conduct their debates in technical terms that would be recognisable to educationalists in many other countries (Paterson 1997). As the Union began to decay in the 1980s and 1990s, the civic leaders of Scottish education played a prominent role in campaigning for a parliament: for example, the main teachers' trade union, the Educational Institute of Scotland, supported and helped to finance the Scotland Forward organisation advocating 'Yes' votes in the 1997 referendum. So education is regarded as commanding cultural authority in Scotland, and has been supposed to be tied to Scotland's sense of identity.

Partly as a result of this, expectations were high in 1997 about the impact which a parliament could have on education (Brown *et al.* 1999: 118). It was not surprising that it was an educational matter – student finance – that became one of the most controversial issues in

the 1999 Scottish election. The outcome was an independent committee of inquiry into the topic, which reported in December 1999
(Independent Committee of Inquiry into Student Finance 1999). As
a result, from autumn 2000 no Scottish students were paying fees on
Scottish higher education courses, and from autumn 2001 new
grants will be introduced to encourage people from low-income
families to take up higher education. The grants will be paid for by,
in effect, a new graduate tax (Scottish Executive 2000). And education
was never far from the headlines in the first year of the Parliament's
operation – controversies not only about fees, but also about teachers'
pay and working conditions, about the rights of sexual minorities in
schools, about the continuing separate existence of publicly-funded
Catholic schools, and about the capacity of the Scottish Qualifications
Authority to manage the school examination system (Paterson
2000d). The educational debate has thus been about the kind of
Scotland over which the new Parliament is presiding.

This prominence given to education in recent political debate
would not be surprising to anyone who had studied the history of
nationalist movements elsewhere. Education has always been at the
heart of nationalist programmes – often as strongly in those which
advocate partial independence for the nation as in projects of national
separation (Gellner 1983; Green 1997; Schleicher 1993). Precisely
because education is linked to renewing the national culture, to
investing in the national economy and to maintaining the civic
institutions which embodied the nation in the absence of national
independence, it has always occupied the attention of the new legislators in newly autonomous national parliaments. In more recent
times, liberal versions of education have been supposed to be especially important to nationalisms that conceive of themselves as civic
(as opposed to ethnic: see Chapter 7). In Catalonia, for example,
education is seen as the means by which immigrants may be
socialised into the Catalan community, learning the language that
would give them the same social rights as the majority (Gore and
MacInnes 2000; Keating 1996: 137–8). In Quebec, the newly civic
nationalism of the period since the 1960s has, likewise, emphasised
the capacity of education to include incomers (Keating 1996: 87–8).

This chapter's concern with education accordingly touches on
some very broad themes. Not all of these can be dealt with in depth,
but they provide part of the context and theory through which we

can understand attitudes to education at a crucial moment in Scotland's history. The chapter is in three parts: in the first, we investigate the extent to which Scottish attitudes to educational policy are different from those in England. On the one hand, as we saw in the previous chapter, attitudes to welfare policy are not much different in the two countries, and so maybe education is not as distinctive an aspect of Scottish identity as is sometimes supposed. On the other hand, the distinctive position of education in Scottish debates may itself have stimulated distinctive attitudes.

In the second part, we then explore in more detail the relationship between people's sense of national identity and their views about educational policy. Is there evidence that a particular constellation of educational views clusters together with a strong sense of Scottishness? And does that relationship mark Scottishness off from the educational aspects of national identity in England?

The final part examines whether views about education relate to opinions about how the Scottish Parliament should evolve. We found in the previous chapter that most political positions on the welfare state had come to focus their expectations on the Parliament. Is that true also of education? Are the political forces pushing towards an extension of the Parliament's powers likely to reinforce (or to weaken) the dominant version of the role which education plays in Scottish national identity?

EDUCATIONAL POLICY IN SCOTLAND AND ENGLAND

Four blocks of questions relating to educational policy were asked in the Scottish Parliamentary Election Survey of 1999 – on the financial aspects of being a student in higher education, on public educational spending, on how to organise an effective system of schools and on the governing context of Scottish education. Most of the first three of these blocks were also asked in the British Social Attitudes Survey of 1999, and so a reliable comparison can be made with England.

Attitudes to student finance are shown in Table 9.1. Scotland seemed to be more enthusiastic about the current expansion of higher education than England. Not only did 52 per cent of Scots want expansion to go further than in 1999, as against 45 per cent of people in England, but they did so from a considerably higher base of participation in higher education: in 1998, the proportion of young people entering higher education by the age of twenty-one was 47 per cent in Scotland, but only about 30 per cent in England (DfEE 1999; Scottish Executive 1999) – although it has to be acknowledged that we cannot be sure that people in Scotland are aware that participation rates are higher in Scotland. Scots also seemed to be somewhat more in favour of public support for students: 46 per cent wanted no students to pay fees, as opposed to 39 per cent in England. Nevertheless, the most impressive feature of Table 9.1 is in fact how similar views were in the two countries, in spite of the claims made in the tuition-fees debate that Scotland was more opposed to fees than England. In both countries, opinion was fairly evenly split on whether fees should be paid by the government, with around half preferring that students pay according to their means. Nearly everyone in Scotland and England wanted a restoration of student grants, and two-thirds of people wanted them to be means tested; under one-third were in favour of students having to borrow money to finance their studies. These views were consistent with the proposals of the independent committee of inquiry into student finance, and with the Scottish government's response, and so we can expect that people in Scotland will be broadly content with the outcome – for a partial restoration of means-tested grants, and for the replacement of upfront fees paid as one lump sum by fees repaid by graduates at a rate proportionate to their earnings. But that was not because the Scottish Parliament addressed distinctive Scottish concerns: it seems to have addressed common British concerns in a distinctively Scottish way.

The responses to questions on educational spending show few differences between Scotland and England (Table 9.2). The most notable, in fact, is that a less strong majority of Scots than of people in England would have made education the first or second priority for government spending: perhaps Scots were aware that education spending per head is already higher in Scotland than in England. Nevertheless, Scots were not averse to the Scottish government's raising taxes to spend on education (59 per cent agree). Generally, people in Scotland and England would have spent public money on the same aspects of education, although Scots were rather more inclined than the English to help students at college (32 per cent as

Table 9.1 Views on higher education policy, Scotland and England

Percentages agreeing	Scotland	England
Increase opportunities to go to higher education*	52	45
Tuition fees paid by government:		
all	46	39
means–tested	50	54
none	3	4
Student grants:		
all	29	28
means–tested	66	67
none	3	3
Student should take out loans	27	31
Sample size (=100%)	1,482	933

*In Scotland, the question referred to 'opportunities in Scotland'.
Sources: Scottish Parliamentary Election Survey 1999; British Social Attitudes Survey 1999

opposed to 23 per cent), maybe reflecting the intensity of the debate about student hardship which accompanied the campaigning on student finance. In both countries, however, most people gave highest priority to the core parts of compulsory education – primary and secondary schooling.

Table 9.2 Views on education spending, Scotland and England

Percentages agreeing	Scotland	England
Education as first or second priority for government spending	62	70*
Scottish government increase taxes for education spending	59	not asked
First or second priority for extra education spending:		
pre-school children	30	28
primary children	47	48
secondary children	46	51
less able children	43	47
college students	32	23
Sample size (=100%)	1,482	933

*sample size 2,722
Sources: Scottish Parliamentary Election Survey 1999; British Social Attitudes Survey 1999

Many aspects of how to manage an effective system of schooling were also viewed in a broadly similar way in Scotland and England (Tables 9.3 and 9.4). The key preferences in both countries were more resources and smaller classes, whether at primary or at secondary level. There is some indication that people in England were more concerned about the quality of secondary teachers than people in Scotland: 37 per cent as opposed to 31 per cent would have given high priority to making teachers more effective. We return later to this point about the standing of teachers in the community. There is some evidence that Scots were more favourably disposed towards the vocational role of secondary education than the English: 36 per cent as opposed to 30 per cent. It has often been argued that the tension between vocational and academic education is not so strong in Scotland as it is in England (Weir 1988; Raffe 1985). A larger difference is found in the roles of comprehensive education and of private education. Two-thirds of Scots were in favour of non-selective secondary schools, but only just over half of people in England. One-quarter of Scots would have abolished private schools altogether (something that would in fact be in contravention of the European Convention on Human Rights), as opposed to 19 per cent of people in England. This Scottish predilection for common schooling is also found in the majority view about Catholic schools: over two-thirds would have ended their publicly funded status, a view shared, in fact,

Table 9.3 Views on effective primary schools,
Scotland and England

Percentages agreeing	Scotland	England
First or second priority for		
improving primary schools:		
more information to parents	2	3
more links with parents	22	18
more resources	42	44
better teachers	30	32
smaller classes	57	59
more child-centred	36	34
better leadership	6	4
Sample size (=100%)	1,482	933

Sources: Scottish Parliamentary Election Survey 1999; British Social Attitudes Survey 1999; British Election Survey 1997

by 42 per cent of Catholics. Since a further 11 per cent of Catholics did not care whether separate schools are maintained by public funds, a majority of Catholics would not have been averse to the ending of that public status.

Table 9.4 Views on effective secondary schools, Scotland and England

Percentages agreeing	Scotland	England
First or second priority for improving secondary schools:		
more information to parents	1	3
more links with parents	13	11
more resources	36	37
better teachers	31	37
smaller classes	36	37
more exams and tests	11	11
more child-centred	27	27
more preparation for work	36	30
better leadership	7	5
Non-selective secondary schools	66	51
Abolish private schools	24	19★
Do not maintain publicly-funded Catholic schools	69	not asked
Sample size (=100%)	1,482	933

★English figure is from 1997, sample size 2,551
Sources: Scottish Parliamentary Election Survey 1999; British Social Attitudes Survey 1999; British Election Survey 1997

At the time of the parliamentary elections, Scots were optimistic about its role in education (Table 9.5): 60 per cent believed that it would increase standards. Despite this view that standards could improve, schools were widely respected as amongst the best-run parts of civic Scotland: 64 per cent of people took this view, a respect only surpassed by that for Scottish banks (78 per cent). This social standing was accorded to the schools, not to the local authorities which have managerial responsibility for them: only 41 per cent of people believed them to be well run.

In summary of this first broad impression of attitudes to the education system, we can say that Scotland is somewhat more favourable than England to public support for education, and to a non-selective

**Table 9.5 Views on the governing context of
Scottish education**

	Percentage agreeing
Scottish Parliament will increase standard of education	60
Scottish institutions well run:	
National Health Service	50
press	55
local government	41
banks	78
trade unions	53
public-sector schools	64
legal system	58
Sample size (=100%)	1,482

Sources: Scottish Parliamentary Election Survey 1999; British Social Attitudes Survey 1999

system of public community schools. Except on selection, however, these national differences in views about education are not much greater than in the views about general social welfare which we analysed in Chapter 8: they are differences of emphasis rather than fundamental disagreements. But, as with social welfare, that broad similarity of attitude does not prevent debates about education taking quite a different turn in Scotland, as the issue of student finance has shown, especially now that the parliament is in charge. Scotland seems to have confidence in the way its education system is run, and to be optimistic about the Scottish Parliament's stewardship of it. We turn next to look at the extent to which education, and these institutions, continue to be viewed as expressing Scottish national identity in this new era.

EDUCATION AND NATIONAL IDENTITY

What constellation of views about education is associated with Scottish identity? In answering this question, we are not seeking to explain how a particular set of educational values comes to be seen as part of Scottishness: doing that requires a more historical approach (Paterson 2000b). The purpose here is to ask simply: what kinds of educational policies are favoured by people who think of themselves as Scottish, and how do these compare with the educational views of people who, in England, see themselves as English?

Table 9.6 shows the relationship between views about educational policy and the respondents' sense of national identity, in Scotland and England. The national identity categories have been condensed from those in the Moreno question that was analysed in Chapter 7. For example, the category 'predominantly Scottish' here includes both 'Scottish not British' and 'more Scottish than British'. The percentages in the table show the level of agreement with each particular aspect of educational policy: for example, in the top left-hand cell, 54 per cent of people who were 'predominantly Scottish' believed that opportunities to go on to higher education should be increased. Only an illustrative selection of educational views is shown in the table.

By contrast with the broad similarity of overall views about educational policy which we noted earlier, the striking general point about Table 9.6 is that Scottish and English national identity had clearly different relationships to education. The question on higher education illustrates this clearly. In Scotland, people who felt Scottish were more likely to support further expansion than people who felt British. In England, the pattern was exactly the opposite: people who felt English were less in favour of expansion than people who felt British. As a result, there were large differences between the views of people who felt Scottish and people who felt English: 54 per cent compared with 41 per cent.

Much the same can be said of all the other items shown in Table 9.6. Giving priority to educational expenditure was associated with feeling Scottish but not with feeling English. On the question of whether the Scottish government should raise taxes to pay for education (not in the table), 62 per cent of people who felt predominantly Scottish agreed, compared with 57 per cent of those who felt equally Scottish and British, and only 42 per cent of those who felt predominantly British. Not surprisingly perhaps, people who felt predominantly Scottish were also more optimistic about the Scottish Parliament's effect on education (62 per cent) than those who felt equally Scottish and British (54 per cent) or predominantly British (50 per cent).

Scottishness, but not Englishness, was strongly associated with support for non-selective secondary schools. Scottishness was associated with favouring more links between schools and parents (whether at primary or secondary level), not an association found in England. Scottishness was strongly associated with respect for teachers: for

**Table 9.6 Views on education policy by national identity*,
Scotland and England**

Percentages agreeing	Scotland			England		
	pre-dominantly Scottish	equally Scottish and British	pre-dominantly British	pre-dominantly English	equally English and British	pre-dominantly British
Increase opportunities to go to higher education**	54	45	44	41	42	51
Education as first or second priority for government spending	38	43	28	34	29	30
Non–selective secondary schools	69	66	45	51	52	51
First or second priority for improving primary schools:						
more links with parents	23	22	16	19	16	20
better teachers	27	35	43	32	26	38
First or second priority for improving secondary schools:						
more links with parents	13	13	7	11	10	13
better teachers	28	35	51	39	33	37
more preparation for work	37	34	23	27	32	32
Sample size (=100%)	986	334	103	880	999	652

* National identity has been condensed into three categories from the five Moreno categories discussed in Chapter 7.
** In Scotland, the question referred to 'opportunities in Scotland'.
Sources: Scottish Parliamentary Election Survey 1999; British Social Attitudes Survey 1999

example, at the secondary level, only 28 per cent of those who felt predominantly Scottish believed that better teachers were needed, in contrast to 35 per cent of those who felt equally Scottish and British and a majority (51 per cent) of the small group who considered themselves to be predominantly British. Scottishness was also associated with support for vocational education in secondary schools.

Thus Table 9.6 does show important national differences, not between Scotland and England, but between the educational components of Scottish and English national identity. The key difference between Scotland and England is not in attitudes to policy, but in how these attitudes relate to national identity. Scottishness is associated with a public system at both school and tertiary level. It is associated with public action to expand opportunities, led by the Scottish Parliament and paid for by taxes. It is associated with a view of schools as part of the community (linking with parents), and with respect for teachers. None of this is true of Englishness, which in some respects is associated with quite opposite views. One consequence is that the educational connotations of Britishness are different in Scotland and England. Britishness in England is somewhat associated with the same public values as are associated with Scottishness in Scotland, whereas Britishness in Scotland is associated with doubts about these values.

That much is perfectly consistent with the literature on education and national identity. But does a national identity constituted partly by support for a public education system prove that Scotland is an unambiguously civic place? As in other countries, we might expect that support for a public system would be associated with an inclusive attitude to citizenship — a belief that education is the means by which a nation socialises newcomers.

In fact, popular views do not neatly distinguish between civic and ethnic national identity, which we find if we look at the relationship between views about education and levels of support for two of the definitions of Scottish citizenship that were analysed in Chapter 7: that it should be granted to anyone born in Scotland (regardless of where they were living), or that it should be granted to anyone living in Scotland (regardless of where they were born). The former view is usually supposed to be a component of ethnic interpretations of nationalism (McCrone 1998: 9) — the *ius sanguinis* of, for example, traditional German identity.

155

In Scotland, supporting a public system of common education was associated with both the civic and the ethnic definition. For example, those who favoured a non-selective system of schooling showed 57 per cent support for the civic view and 82 per cent for the ethnic, each at least as high as the support among people who favoured a selective system. People who admired the way in which civic Scotland is run were, certainly, more inclined to support a civic view of identity than those who had doubts about civic Scotland. But the admirers were also no less likely – and usually more likely – than the sceptics to support an ethnic view of citizenship as well.

The popularity in Scotland of education's role in creating a civic view of identity can be reinforced with evidence from other sources. For example, research carried out by the OECD with a Scottish sample size of 810 (Scottish Office 1995), found that 86 per cent of people in Scotland wanted schools to teach pupils how to be good citizens (a level of support that was higher than in nearly all other OECD countries). Part of that was teaching students to live among people of different backgrounds: Scottish support for that (84 per cent) was higher than in England and Wales, although in line with the OECD average. These points are consistent with the belief that education can create a community partly by socialising incomers. On the other hand, there was relatively low support (55 per cent) in Scotland for teaching about other parts of the world, lower in fact than in all other OECD countries apart from England and Wales.

These popular views show that we should not exaggerate the distinction between civic and ethnic. Hearn (2000: 194) puts this well:

> In the Scottish case, nationalism's civicness is culturally determined. . . . This is not to say that it is irrational, but simply that its rationality . . . is culturally embedded, transmitted and sustained.

Our analysis can also be read in this light. Education, as an institution that is very much concerned with cultural transmission, is both a means by which incomers are brought into the national community and a way in which that community's values are sustained. The inclusiveness of the Scottish moral community is clearly seen in the levels of support for a public system of common education. But, by the very fact of being associated with Scottish national identity, that community becomes an ethnic fact about Scottishness, and therefore potentially excluding of those who – despite the open invitation to do so – refuse to identify with Scottishness.

So the conclusion we would draw from this analysis of education and national identity is that, although attitudes to education are not fundamentally different in Scotland and England, they are seen through a national or even nationalist prism in Scotland, and so their effects may be radically different. That is one reason why the debate on tuition fees took off: they were seen, probably, as an attack on the putatively democratic character of Scotland's universities. Therefore, if, as we argued in Chapters 3, 4, 6 and 7, elections to Holyrood emphasise that nationalist prism, then being seen to run Scottish education effectively and in ways that are consistent with Scottish traditions might prove effective electorally.

EDUCATION AND THE SCOTTISH PARLIAMENT

If Scottish education is linked to the definition of Scottish identity, we might expect views about education to be associated with people's views of the Parliament. Generally, those who most favoured the most Scottish views on education – in other words, who favoured a public system of education – were most inclined to be optimistic about the Parliament's impact. We now look at whether these same educational preferences incline people to want the Parliament's powers to be extended.

It is indeed true that people who supported a public system of education were more favourable to extending the Parliament's powers than those who had some doubts about that. Thus extending the powers was strongly associated with support for expanding opportunities in higher education, with publicly funded fees and students' receiving grants. Extending powers was associated with favouring increased taxes for educational expenditure, and with education's being a high priority for public expenditure. Extending powers was also associated with favouring non-selective schools, and with wanting to abolish private schools.

Views about Catholic schools differed in a relevant way between Catholics and non-Catholics. Among Catholics, support for the Parliament's having stronger powers was higher (69 per cent) among people who wanted the ending of publicly-funded Catholic schools than among those who wanted to maintain these (63 per cent). So

157

Catholics followed the general pattern we have been noting: those in favour of a common system of schooling were more in favour of a stronger parliament. Among Protestants and among people with no religious affiliation, however, the pattern was the other way round. The highest support for a stronger parliament was among those who did not favour the abolition of publicly funded Catholic schools. (There were too few people of non-Christian religion in the survey to allow a reliable assessment to be made of their views.) In a sense, though, these patterns, too, confirm the general point. For non-Catholics to favour the retention of Catholic schools could be interpreted as a commitment to an inclusive education system, and so it could be argued that, for non-Catholics too, the more educationally inclusive response was, again, the more in favour of an increase in the Parliament's powers.

Support for an increase in the Parliament's powers was, unsurprisingly, highest among those who thought that the Parliament would be good for education. It was also highest among people who were somewhat less impressed by the governance of civic institutions. For example, among people who thought public-sector schools are well run, 57 per cent favoured more powers; the proportion among people who thought they are not well run is 61 per cent. So there seems to be some support for the claim by campaigners for a parliament that one of its purposes should be to reform civic Scotland, including the governance of education. The only aspect of civic life where that was not true was local government, probably because to trust the Parliament to achieve things requires that people trusted the only other indigenous elected politicians as well.

Favouring a public education system, and expecting the Parliament to reform the governance of civic Scotland, seemed to encourage people to want to extend the Parliament's powers. Nevertheless, as in the analysis in Chapter 8 of social welfare, a more generally striking feature here is that nearly all views are consistent with favouring more powers for the Parliament: in all but one case, a majority takes that position. The exception is people who did not expect the Parliament to improve education, but even there the group who wanted the Parliament's powers extended (44 per cent) was larger than those who wanted the powers curtailed (35 per cent). So, as for social welfare generally, the politics of Scottish education at the time of the May 1999 election were becoming focused on the new parliament.

The Parliament was not simply a device to achieve specific policy goals, but was the forum in which a variety of views about policy could be debated.

CONCLUSION

The main point we have made in this chapter is that Scottish national identity is associated in distinctive ways with views about education. Scottishness is associated with seeing education as a publicly-funded resource for the community, commanding public respect and including incomers into the community. Englishness is broadly associated with the opposite values. In England, indeed, Britishness is associated with educational values which in Scotland are probably seen as Scottish, while – to some extent – Britishness in Scotland is associated with English values. The weakness of a common British culture is evident in these patterns. Not only are Scottishness and Englishness quite distinct in their educational implications. As a consequence of this, Britishness itself is taking on quite different meanings in the two countries.

We are not claiming any causal link here between education and national identity. The matter is too complex to say simply that feeling Scottish causes support for a public education system, or that supporting such a system induces people to identify with the Scottishness which it embodies; almost certainly, the causal links go in both directions. All that our survey results can do is point to a clustering of views that help to define the meaning of Scottish identity (or of English or British identity): a feature of Scottishness is that it goes along with support for a public education system.

That is broadly why the Scottish Parliament is now seen in Scotland as the route by which the education system can be improved. Because the Parliament embodies the public and political aspects of identity, it is becoming the natural place to govern the public aspects of identity's civic manifestations, such as the education system. The Parliament may be a thoroughly modern institution, the views of identity in Scotland may be largely pluralistic (as we saw in attitudes towards citizenship in Chapter 7), and the education system may be mostly governed in its daily operation by the internationally familiar technical debates that govern education everywhere in the developed world. But underlying all this is a deeper and more familiar old story: the relationship between identity, education and parliament in Scotland provides a perfect instance of a classic tale in the history of nationalism.

10

CONCLUSION:
THE FUTURE OF SCOTTISH
POLITICS

—·····ʀʀᴘⓅᴀʀʀ····—

INTRODUCTION

It has become a cliché in Scotland, as in Wales, that self-government is a process not an event. But that tells us nothing about what kind of process it is, or will be, what route it will take, and what destination people imagine they are aiming for, even though also being open to the distinct possibility that there is no firm destination at all. Our analysis in this book offers some indications of how these questions can be answered. More than in the immediate aftermath of the referendum, and far more than in the distant days just five years ago when a Scottish Parliament still seemed a very remote prospect, it is possible to see the new politics of Scotland emerging, and a series of surveys such as we have analysed here is an excellent way of painting this picture.

So in this concluding chapter we consider the future under four broad headings – political parties, social policy, the constitution and culture. For each of these, we summarise what our book has had to say on the questions of whether a new Scottish politics is emerging, and whether there is a new Scottish public underpinning the constitutional reforms.

POLITICAL PARTIES

The main party questions concern Labour, for the reasons we have already outlined in Chapter 8. Labour has been so dominant in Scottish politics for so long that the movements of opinion that matter are all away from it. In particular, if the SNP is ever going to break through, then they have to take some ten percentage points from Labour, and so who these voters are and what their motivation for switching parties might be is of critical importance. The questions of the fate of the Tories and the Liberal Democrats may become important in the future, not least because they both seem to be consolidating their positions even though not making great advances; as yet, though, they remain on the sidelines.

So what has our survey analysis suggested is happening to the Labour vote? The most striking first impression is of disappointment. People had enormous hopes for the first Labour government in eighteen years – especially since Labour had in fact won every Scottish election in the meantime – and so disappointment was probably inevitable. But there has also been a sense that the Blair government has been exceptionally uninspiring. It is widely perceived as having moved to the right, leaving the largest segment of Scottish opinion – nearly a majority – now to the left of it. Trust in Labour to look after working-class interests has declined sharply, as has trust in them to look after Scottish interests. When we remember how the Tories suffered in the 1980s and 1990s from being seen as an anti-Scottish party, the lessons for Labour seem stark.

That is an opportunity for the SNP and for the Scottish Socialist Party. We have seen that in 1999 Labour was already losing left-wing defectors to both of them, and for the first time ever the largest group of Scottish voters viewed the SNP as being to the left of Labour. At the same time, Labour was not gaining votes on the right. Indeed, Labour's rightwards drift seems not to have benefited the party much at all, and may actually have driven some people who share that ideological view into the hands of the Liberal Democrats and (rather oddly) the SNP. Nevertheless, if Labour can stem the drift and keep its support above about one-third of the vote, then it will remain the largest party because its vote is so efficiently concentrated into the first-past-the-post contests it can win. If the SNP is to become a governing party, then it must start gaining these: it will never break through on the regional votes alone. Indeed, if the SNP can make large gains in the first-past-the-post part of the Holyrood elections, then the growing strength of the SSP will start to work in their favour. Labour, losing constituency seats to the SNP, would also lose regional seats to the SSP. That is the circumstance under which Labour would collapse, but the sheer difficulty for the SNP in making these constituency gains is also a measure of how secure Labour seems to be.

POLICY

The party battle is about image and ideology, and not necessarily about policy directly, but policy debates are the terrain on which the conflicts are fought. Our analysis is yet another confirmation that Scottish views about social policy are not substantially more left-wing than those in England, mainly because English views are clearly social democratic as well. Scotland and England also seem broadly favourable to the Blair government's programme of modernising the welfare state. There are some notable exceptions to this – especially in attitudes to education – but the broad agreement is what is striking.

But the politics of it all are very different. That is sometimes a matter of rhetoric: for example, even though Scotland and England agree that wealth is unequally distributed in society and that that is unfair, the politically loaded term 'redistribution' seems to be much less off-putting in Scotland than in England. Rhetoric then translates into the party conflicts. In England, Labour has that left-of-centre majority at its disposal, and seems to be in little immediate danger of losing its allegiance permanently. In Scotland, it is competing for these votes with the SNP and the SSP.

More fundamentally, whereas English social democrats have only the Labour party governing at Westminster to hang on to, in Scotland there always remains the possibility of pushing the devolved Parliament towards greater independence if Westminster seems not to be delivering the social-democratic policy preferences they favour. But the link between views about policy and the evolution of the Scottish Parliament is more subtle than that, because people who are not on the left also favour an extension of the Parliament's powers. It seems that the Parliament was already, in 1999, being seen as the main forum for debating the future of Scottish social policy, regardless of the present settlement of powers between it and Westminster.

THE CONSTITUTION

And so the constitutional question will not go away. Of course, before thinking about the future, we have to start with the questions about how Scots reacted to their first-ever opportunity to vote for a domestic parliament. There was quite a high rate of abstention (although not higher than that in elections to similar autonomous parliaments in other parts of Europe), and the people who voted differed in important ways from those who did not. Probably the most telling difference for predicting the future is that people who voted were more likely than those who abstained to see the Parliament as central to Scottish politics. This is going to be a perennial problem for Unionists, and an opportunity for nationalists. The relatively low turnout also shows that merely setting up a new devolved institution has not galvanised the people of Scotland into democratic participation: what could be called the Charter 88 agenda, of renewing democracy, needs more than merely institutional reform.

That said, people still have an optimistic view about the possibility of the Parliament's renewing Scottish democracy: they expect it to give ordinary people a stronger voice in government. Future surveys will allow us to assess whether that optimism has survived the controversies over accountability that dominated the Parliament's first year. Did people feel that the compromise over repealing Section 2a showed that the policy process is sufficiently responsive, or did they feel that the mere fact of repeal – apparently against majority opinion – betrayed a political class that is out of touch? In the aftermath of the disastrous performance of the Scottish Qualifications Authority in summer 2000 – issuing wrong results to school students – did people feel that the report of the Parliament's education committee did a good job on drawing the wider lesson for the accountability of quangos and government ministers (Paterson 2000d)? Very practical issues such as these show that abstract questions of the constitution and accountability can indeed exercise popular concern.

The complications of this continuing process of constitutional reform for Labour arise partly because of the new proportional electoral system. People seem to have liked the experience, and to have been encouraged by it. There is widespread understanding of the role of the two ballots, although less understanding of how the votes are then translated into seats.

Nevertheless, novel though this institution and the voting system are, it looks as if the voters were using them in a very familiar way – as yet another institutional tool with which to put pressure on Westminster to respect Scottish interests. They have been doing that with local and Westminster elections and parties throughout the three centuries of the Union, and so it is perhaps not surprising that they should use this new institution in a similar manner. The embedding of the Parliament into the national consciousness is best shown in the view of it now taken by people who used to be sceptical about it – Tories, and people who regard themselves as British. Both groups now accept the Parliament, presumably seeing it as the means to represent Scottish interests in the Union just as the Scottish Office and various civic bodies have done in the past.

So it is also not surprising that Scots in general seem already to be thinking about how to fashion that tool in ways that, they believe, would better express Scottish interests. There is a more realistic view about what this kind of parliament can achieve, and a clear majority preference for it to have the powers that would enable it to do more. It is more trusted than Westminster to look after Scottish interests, and indeed is seen in the long term as much more relevant to Scotland than Westminster.

At the same time, domesticated though the Parliament seems to have become, it is not seen as inevitably leading to Scottish independence. The constitutional pragmatism that has characterised Scottish views throughout the period of Union seems still to hold. Even though a majority wants a stronger parliament, only a minority actually favours independence. The majority is not hostile to independence, but wants to wait and see.

CULTURE

Our analysis has also confirmed the longstanding finding that questions of cultural identity are only loosely linked to political questions in Scotland. Despite the rhetoric of nationalism, it is impossible to infer massive support for independence from the fact that most people in Scotland feel intensely Scottish. And, despite what Union-ists say, the continuing attachment to cultural Britishness does not tell us anything very much about the long-term prospects for the Union.

There has been a strengthening of Scottishness in the last two decades, and a declining willingness to identify with Britishness. But identity is fluid. Scottishness peaked during the 1997 referendum, and fell back by 1999, although not back to the levels it was at before (which were already very high). People have a fairly pluralistic view of what makes a 'Scot', a majority being open to that title's being conferred on anyone residing in Scotland, even though a bigger majority is ready to grant Scottishness to people born in Scotland. The view seems to be that people can stack up claims to identity – birth, current residence, ancestry – and that the higher the pile the stronger the claim. What definitely seems not to be the case is that any particular brick in the stack is an absolutely necessary prerequisite.

People actually switch their 'identity', placing different emphasis on the Scottish and British components according to circumstance. The problem for our analysis is that the precise nature of these cir-cumstances is not at all clear. The balance between Scottish and British varies in ways that are mostly not related to demographic, political or social views. Maybe it's just idiosyncratic – what appears in statistical modelling as random – and so maybe we should be casting doubt on that apparently stable word 'identity'.

Saying that this changing sense of nationality has no political implications would be too strong. After all, there is a growing sense that Scotland and England are in conflict with each other, and a growing willingness also to identify with people of the same nation-ality who are in a different social class, by contrast with people in the other country who are in the same class. But the political expressions of nationality are not explicitly cultural. They appear in a particular constellation of views about social policy – for example, the apparent Scottish view that education should be a public good that promotes equal opportunity, and that is staffed by teachers who are held in high public regard. These views then are mobilised at election time and influence policy – such as the change to the regime of student finance. The new policy is different from that in the rest of the UK, and so identity has played a part in formulating policy, even though identity is not directly political and even though Scottish views on student finance are not much different from views in England and Wales.

CONCLUSION

There is currently a real sense in Scotland that everything is changing, that nothing can be taken for granted. Some social attitudes that would normally alter only slowly have taken apparently wild swings in the last few years – for example, the expectations of the new parliament. The country is going through the closest to a social revolution that can be found in a developed western democracy.

There is, then, a methodological conclusion to be drawn from the analysis we have presented in this book. The only way to understand what is happening is by means of regular national surveys of the kind we have been reporting. Opinion polls are excellent ways of capturing the mood of the moment, but there is no substitute for continuity over time when trying to understand the underlying changes. Similarly, focus groups may help political parties to track short-term swings in views about leaders or policy. But only the rigorously generalisable results of statistical analysis can allow us to make valid statements about society as whole.

And the long-term and generalisable statements we would make finally on this occasion are these. The Scottish Parliament has become the main forum for Scottish politics. It may or may not evolve eventually into an independent state, but people in Scotland expect it to become stronger as time goes on. Even with its present powers, it is, quite simply, the forum where debates about party politics, social policy and nationality are played out. The next UK general election in Scotland will, therefore, also be about the Scottish Parliament; it will be about which parties can best help that institution to represent Scottish interests at the heart of the UK state. The overriding question of Scottish politics now, and for the foreseeable future, is how well the current home rule settlement articulates Scottish views to the wider world.

APPENDIX

—⸺◦⸺—

TECHNICAL ASPECTS OF THE SURVEYS

This Appendix includes information about the surveys from which data in the book are drawn, classifications used in the book and data interpretation.

Most data in the book are drawn from the 1999 Scottish Parliamentary Election Survey. This was the first year of the study which in future years will run under the name of the Scottish Social Attitudes Survey, parallel to the long-established British Social Attitudes Survey (Jowell *et al.* 1999a). Other surveys from which data have been used are the Scottish Election Surveys of 1979, 1992 and 1997, the British Election Panel Study which began in 1997 and the 1997 Scottish Referendum Survey. Data from all the surveys are, or will be, publicly available through the Data Archive at the University of Essex.

DETAILS OF THE 1999 SCOTTISH PARLIAMENTARY ELECTION SURVEY

The study was funded by the Economic and Social Research Council (grant number R000238065). The survey involved a face-to-face interview with 1482 respondents and a self-completion questionnaire completed by 1165 of these people. Copies of the questionnaires are available from the National Centre for Social Research, web site www.natcen.ac.uk

Sample design

The Scottish Parliamentary Election Survey was designed to yield a representative sample of adults aged eighteen or over in Scotland. People were eligible for the survey if they were aged eighteen when the interviewer first made contact with them, even if they had not been eighteen on 6 May when the parliamentary election took place. The sampling frame for the survey was the Postcode Address File (PAF), a list of addresses (or postal delivery points) compiled by the Post Office.

For practical reasons, the sample was confined to those living in private households. People living in institutions (such as nursing homes or hospitals – though not in private households at such institutions) were excluded, as were households whose addresses were not on the Postcode Address File. The sampling method involved a multi-stage design, with three separate stages of selection: selection of sectors, addresses and individuals:

1 At the first stage, postcode sectors were selected systematically from a list of all postal sectors in Scotland. Before selection, any sectors with fewer than 500 addresses were identified and grouped together with an adjacent sector. Sectors were then stratified on the basis of grouped council areas,[1] population density (with variable banding used, in order to create three equal-sized strata per sub-region) and percentage of household heads recorded as employers/managers (from the 1991 Census).

Ninety postcode sectors were selected, with probability proportional to the number of addresses in each sector.

2 Thirty-two addresses were initially selected at random in each of the ninety sectors, more than was necessary, but sufficient to allow deselection of any addresses found to be extreme outliers (for example one address on an otherwise non-visited island). As it was, none of the selected addresses was found to be inaccessible and eighty addresses were thus deselected at random from the sample – no more than one address was deselected from each point.

In some places more than one accommodation space shares an address. The Multiple Occupancy Indicator (MOI) on the Postcode Address File shows whether this is known to be the case. If the MOI indicated more than one accommodation space at a given address, the chances of the given address being selected from the list of addresses was increased to match the total number of accommodation spaces. As would be expected, the majority (91 per cent) of MOIs had a value of one. The remainder, which ranged between three and twenty, were incorporated into the weighting procedures (described below). In some places (predominantly tenement flats), the MOI was found by the interviewer to be incorrect and additional random sampling of addresses was carried out manually to correct for this. In total, ten new addresses were added to the sample in this way.

In total, the sample comprised 2810 addresses across ninety sampling points and each sample point issued to interviewers contained thirty-one or thirty-two addresses.

3 Interviewers called at each selected address and listed all those eligible for inclusion in the sample – that is, all persons currently aged eighteen or over and resident at the selected address. The interviewer then selected one respondent using a computer-generated random selection procedure.

Weighting

Data were weighted to take account of the fact that not all the units covered in the survey had the same probability of selection. The weighting reflected the relative selection probabilities of the individual at the three main stages of selection: address, household and individual.

First, because addresses were selected using the Multiple Output Indicator (MOI), weights had to be applied to compensate for the greater probability of an address with an MOI of more than one being selected, compared to an address with an MOI of one. Secondly, data were weighted to compensate for the fact that dwelling units at an address which contained a large number of dwelling units were less likely to be selected for inclusion in the survey than ones which did not share an address. (We used this procedure because in most cases these two stages will cancel each other out, resulting in more efficient weights). Thirdly, data were weighted to compensate for the lower selection probabilities of adults living in large households compared with those living in small households. All weights fell within a range between 0.05 and 6.0. The weighted sample was scaled down to make the number of weighted productive cases exactly equal to the number of unweighted productive cases.

All the percentages presented in this book are based on weighted data; unweighted samples sizes are shown in the tables.

Fieldwork

Interviewing was carried out between May and August 1999 (92 per cent of interviews being completed by the end of June). An advance letter telling people living at selected addresses that an interviewer would call was sent out before the interviewers called.

Fieldwork was conducted by interviewers drawn from the National Centre's regular panel and conducted using face-to-face computer-assisted interviewing. (Computer-assisted interviewing involves the use of laptop computers during the interview, with questions appearing on the computer screen and interviewers entering responses directly into the computer.) Interviewers attended a one-day briefing conference to familiarise them with the questionnaires and procedures for selecting addresses and individuals to interview.

The average interview length was 56 minutes. Interviews recorded as taking less than 20 minutes or more than 180 minutes were excluded as they were likely to reflect recording errors. Interviewers achieved an overall response rate of 59 per cent. Details are shown below:

	No.	%
Addresses issued[1]	2,810	
Vacant, derelict and other out of scope	317	
In scope	2,493	100.0
Interview achieved	1,482	59.4
Interview not achieved	1,011	40.6
Refused[2]	672	30.7
Non-contacted[3]	166	3.6
Other non-response	173	6.6

[1] Includes ten addresses identified by interviewers during fieldwork.

[2]'Refusals' comprise refusals before selection of an individual at the address, refusals to the office, refusal by the selected person, 'proxy' refusals (on behalf of the selected respondent) and broken appointments after which the selected person could not be contacted again.

[3]'Non-contacts' comprise households where no one was contacted and those where the selected person could not be contacted.

All respondents were asked to fill in a self-completion questionnaire which, whenever possible, was collected by the interviewer, but in some cases was posted to the National Centre. Up to three postal reminders were sent to obtain the maximum number of self-completion supplements.

A total of 317 respondents (21 per cent of those interviewed) did not return their self-completion questionnaire. We judged that it was not necessary to apply additional weights to correct for this non-response.

OTHER SURVEYS USED IN THE BOOK

Scottish Election Surveys

Scottish Election Surveys have been carried out as part of a series of British Election Surveys undertaken in 1974, 1979, 1992 and 1997. The British Election Surveys, which have been conducted since 1964, take place immediately after each general election. Since the 1970s, the Economic and Social Research Council (ESRC) has been involved in funding each of these surveys (other funders for some surveys have included the Gatsby Foundation – one of the Sainsbury family charitable trusts – and Pergamon Press). The surveys have been directed by various people and organisations over the years, most recently the Centre for Research into Elections and Social Trends (CREST), an ESRC funded research centre linking the National Centre for Social Research and Nuffield College, Oxford (see Thomson *et al.* (1999) for more details). Since November 1999, CREST has moved from Nuffield College to the Department of Sociology, University of Oxford.

In this book we use data from the 1979, 1992 and 1997 Scottish Election Surveys. Fieldwork and data preparation for the 1992 and 1997 surveys were carried out by the National Centre for Social Research (then called Social and Community Planning Research). The Scottish samples were boosted in each of these years to allow data to be analysed for Scotland independently of Britain. The samples for each study were chosen using random selection modified by stratification and clustering. Up to 1992, the sampling frame was the electoral register (ER); in 1997 it was the Postcode Address File (PAF). Weights can be applied to make the 1997 survey (PAF) comparable with the previous (ER) samples.

Achieved sample sizes for Scotland were:

1979   729   (response rate 61 per cent)
1992   957   (response rate 74 per cent)
1997   882   (response rate 62 per cent)

Weighting of the data was carried out in each year to take account of unequal selection probabilities. The surveys involved self-completion supplements in 1992 and 1997, while in 1979 face-to-face interviews were carried out in people's homes, supplemented by a self-completion questionnaire returned after the interview.

Scottish Referendum Survey

The Scottish Referendum Survey (alongside a comparative Welsh Referendum Survey) was undertaken in September–October 1997, funded by the ESRC (grant no. M5443/285/001) and directed by CREST. Fieldwork was carried out by the National Centre for Social Research and interviewing began immediately after the referendum.

The sample was designed to be representative of the adult population who were living in private households in Scotland and eligible to vote in the referendum. It was drawn from the PAF and involved stratification and clustering. Weighting of the data was subsequently carried out to correct for variable selection probabilities.

The survey involved a face-to-face interview, administered using a traditional paper questionnaire, and a self-completion questionnaire. A total of 676 interviews were carried out, a response rate of 68 per cent. Self-completion questionnaires were obtained from 657 respondents (97 per cent of those interviewed). For more information on the survey, see Thomson *et al.* (2000).

British Election Panel Study (BEPS)

After the 1992 and 1997 elections, respondents to the British Election Survey of that year (including those in the Scottish booster sample) were followed up with interviews at least once a year until the next general election. Data from the study beginning in 1997 (BEPS–2) are included in this book. Again, funding for the study was provided by the ESRC, the survey was directed by CREST and fieldwork was undertaken by the National Centre for Social Research. The purpose of creating a panel of people to follow over time is that the evolution of attitudes can be tracked. However, this is only reliable if attrition (that is, the loss of members of the sample over time) does not distort the sample. The following analyses suggest that in this case the 1999 wave of the panel study does provide a reasonably accurate picture of the evolution of the views of the people who were in the 1997 election survey.

Seventy-one per cent of respondents involved in the 1997 British Election Study also took part in the 1999 wave of the panel study. This rate did not vary much between different types of respondents in 1997, as measured by their sex, social class (Goldthorpe Classification: see below), age, nation of the UK, or general election vote in 1997. Including all these variables in a logistic regression predicting the chances of taking part in the 1999 survey found only two statistically significant influences, social class and age. The social class effect reflects the higher than average attrition of people who had never had a job. Their response rate in 1999 was just 53 per cent, but since they comprised only 3 per cent of the total sample their under-representation in 1999 will not have had a strongly distorting effect on the shape of the sample. The age effect on response reflects the higher than average attrition of older people (and the youngest members of the sample), but the differences were not large in absolute terms. Thus the proportion replying in 1999 was 66 per cent among those aged 18–34, 76 per cent for ages 35–50, 78 per cent for ages 51–65 and 64 per cent for ages 66 or older.

The most encouraging point for our analysis is that there was no statistically significant difference in response rates between parties: the rates were 78 per cent for Conservatives, 72 per cent for Labour, 77 per cent for Liberal Democrat and (in Scotland) 76 per cent for the SNP. In Scotland, there was also no difference in response rates among categories of views about the most desirable constitutional future for Scotland: the response rates were 74 per cent among those favouring independence, 71 per cent for supporters of a parliament with taxation powers, 75 per cent for supporters of a parliament without taxation powers, and 74 per cent of opponents of any kind of parliament. The same was true of categories of national identity in Scotland: the response rates were 72 per cent among people who described themselves as 'Scottish not British', 74 per cent for 'Scottish more than British', 67 per cent for 'Scottish equal to British', and 71 per cent for the remaining categories combined.

British Social Attitudes Survey

The BSAS has been running annually since 1983. It aims to yield a representative sample of adults aged eighteen and over living in Britain. Since 1993, the sampling frame has been the Postcode Address File. The sample is selected by methods similar to those used in the election surveys. The sample size has generally been between 3000 and 3500, of whom about 300–350 are in Scotland. The purpose of the surveys is to go beyond the work of opinion polls to collect information underlying changes in people's attitudes and values. Further information on the BSAS is contained in each of the annual reports on it: for the two surveys used in Chapter 8 (1998 and 1999), see Jowell *et al.* (1998, 1999a).

CLASSIFICATIONS USED IN ANALYSIS

Social class/socio-economic group

Social class classifications are derived from people's occupations. Respondents on the Scottish Parliament Election Survey were classified according either to their own occupation or to that of their spouse/partner. Spouse/partner's job details were collected if the respondent was not economically active or retired, while their spouse/partner was economically active or retired. Otherwise respondent's job details were collected (unless never worked). In this book two classifications are used, socio-economic group and the Goldthorpe Schema.

Socio-economic Group (SEG) aims to bring together people with jobs of similar social and economic status, and is derived from a combination of employment status and occupation. The full SEG classification identifies eighteen categories, but these are usually condensed into six groups:

- Professionals, employers and managers
- Intermediate non-manual workers
- Junior non-manual workers
- Skilled manual workers
- Semi-skilled manual workers
- Unskilled manual workers

The remaining respondents are grouped as 'never had a job' or 'not classifiable'. Further collapsing of the classification can classify people as being in 'non-manual' or 'manual' socio-economic groups.

The Goldthorpe schema classifies occupations by their 'general comparability', considering such factors as sources and levels of income, economic security, promotion prospects and level of job autonomy and authority. The Goldthorpe schema was derived from the OPCS Standard Occupational Classification (SOC) combined with employment status. Two versions of the schema are coded: the full schema has eleven categories; the 'compressed schema' combines these into the five classes shown below:

- Salariat (professional and managerial)
- Routine non-manual workers (office and sales)
- Petty bourgeoisie (the self-employed, including farmers, with and without employees)
- Manual foremen and supervisors
- Working class (skilled, semi-skilled and unskilled manual workers, personal service and agricultural workers)

There is a residual category comprising those who have never had a job or who gave insufficient information for classification purposes.

PARTY IDENTIFICATION

Respondents were classified as identifying with a particular political party if they considered themselves supporters of that party, or as closer to it than to others. This is the British Election Survey (BES) classification. The British Social Attitudes Survey (BSA) also includes people who say they would be more likely to support a party in the event of a general election.

NATIONAL IDENTITY

The survey uses a scale, known as the Moreno scale, to measure how people relate being Scottish and being British, if at all. Single identities, either Scottish or British, form the ends of the scale and these identities are equal at the mid-point. At points 2 and 4, one or other is stressed but both are included. The question asks:

Which, if any, of the following best describes how you see yourself?
Scottish, not British
More Scottish than British

Equally Scottish and British
More British than Scottish
British, not Scottish
None of these.

A second survey measure also used is a simpler question which asks respondents to select one identity from a list, which best describes them. They are asked:

If you had to choose, which one *best* describes the way you think of yourself?
British
English
European
Irish
Northern Irish
Scottish
Welsh
None of these.

Attitude scales

The Scottish Parliamentary Election Survey included four attitude scales. The first two scales developed by Heath *et al.* (1994) aim to measure where respondents stand on certain underlying value dimensions. They are a left–right (socialist–*laissez-faire*) scale and a liberal–authoritarian scale. Versions of the attitudes scales have been used since the 1986 BSA and 1987 BES. In addition to these two scales two further scales, measuring British nationalism and Scottish nationalism respectively, are used (Heath *et al.* 1999). Each scale consists of an aggregation of individual survey items designed to measure different aspects of the underlying belief system. A useful way of summarising the information from a number of questions of this sort is to construct an additive index (DeVellis, 1991; Spector, 1992). This approach rests on the assumption that there is an underlying – 'latent' – attitudinal dimension which characterises the answers to all the questions within each scale. If so, scores on the index are likely to be a more reliable indication of the underlying attitude than the answers to any one question.

The socialist–*laissez-faire*, liberal–authoritarian and British nationalism scales each consist of six survey items and can therefore take values ranging from 6–30 (each item has responses 1–5 ranging from agree strongly to disagree strongly). The Scottish nationalism scale attempts to mirror the British scale but has only five items and can, therefore, take values from 5–25.

The items are (with the variable names in the data set) are:

Left–right scale/socialist–laissez-faire scale
- Ordinary working people get their fair share of the nation's wealth [FairShar]
- There is one law for the rich and one for the poor [RichLaw]
- There is no need for strong trade unions to protect employees' working conditions and wages [TuntNeed]
- Private enterprise is the best way to solve Britain's economic problems [PrivEnt]
- Major public services and industries ought to be in state owner-ship [PublcOwn]
- It is the government's responsibility to provide a job for every-one who wants one [GovResp1]

Liberal–authoritarian scale
- People should be allowed to organise public meetings to protest against the government [PubMeet]
- Homosexual relations are always wrong [Gaysex]
- People in Britain should be more tolerant of those who lead unconventional lives [Tolerant]
- Political parties which wish to overthrow democracy should be allowed to stand in general elections [BanParty]
- Young people today don't have enough respect for Britain's traditional values [TradVals]
- Censorship of films and magazines is necessary to uphold moral standards [Censor]

British nationalism scale
- Britain has a lot to learn from other countries in running its affairs [NatLearn]
- I would rather be a citizen of Britain than any other country in the world [NatCitzn]
- There are some things about Britain today that make me ashamed to be British [NatAshmd]
- People in Britain are too ready to criticise their country [NatCrit]

- The government of Britain should do everything it can to keep all parts of Britain together in a single state [NatState]
- Britain should co-operate with other countries, even if it means giving up some independence [NatCoop]

Scottish nationalism scale
- Scotland has a lot to learn from the rest of Britain in running its affairs [SwLearn]
- I would rather be living in Scotland than in any other country in the world [SwLiv]
- There are some things about Scotland today that make me ashamed to be Scottish [SwAshmd]
- People in Scotland are too ready to criticise their country [SwCrit]
- Scotland can only really feel proud of itself if it becomes an independent country [SwProud]

Low values on the scales represent the socialist, liberal and nationalist positions respectively.

The scales have been tested for reliability (as measured by Cronbach's alpha). Values of 0.94 were obtained for both the left–right scale and the liberal–authoritarian scale in 1999. This level of reliability can be considered 'very good' (DeVellis 1991). The nationalism scales were less reliable: the British nationalism scale had a Cronbach's alpha value of 0.45 and for the Scottish nationalism scale the value was 0.36.

DATA INTERPRETATION

Statistical significance

All the data in the book come from samples of the population, meaning that they are subject to sampling error. However, it is possible to calculate confidence intervals relating to any value from a given sample, creating a range within which we can have a certain level of confidence that the true population value lies. Table A.1 gives an indication of the confidence intervals that apply to different percentage results for different sample sizes. Ninety-five per cent confidence intervals are shown, meaning that we can be 95 per cent sure that the true answer lies within the range shown. For example, for a result of 50 per cent based on a sample of 500 there is a 95 per cent chance that the true result lies within ± 4 per cent (thus, between 46 per cent and 54 per cent).

Table A.1 Confidence intervals for survey findings

Sample size	Approximate 95% confidence limits for a percentage result of:		
	10% or 90% +/−	30% or 70% +/−	50% +/−
50	8	13	14
100	6	9	10
250	4	6	6
500	3	4	4
1,000	2	3	3
2,000	1	2	2

These confidence limits assume a simple random sample with no adjustment made for the effects of clustering the sample into a number of sample points. Although such an adjustment would increase the confidence limits slightly, in most cases these would not differ notably from those shown in the table (Paterson 2000c: Appendix). It should be noted that certain types of variables (those most associated with the area where a person lives) are more affected by clustering than others. For example, Labour identifiers and local authority tenants tend to be concentrated in certain areas and consequently the confidence intervals around such variables would widen more were the effect of the sample being clustered taken into account, than would be the case for many attitudinal variables (Jowell *et al.* 1999a).

Tests of statistical significance take account of the confidence intervals attached to survey findings. They can be carried out using modelling techniques (such as that described below), or by hand. Whenever comments on differences between sub-groups of the sample are made in this book, these differences have been tested and found to be statistically significant at the 5 per cent level or stronger. Similarly, although standard deviations are not always presented alongside mean figures in this book, these have been calculated and used to verify the statistical significance of the differences between mean figures which are commented on.

Statistical modelling

For many of the more complex analyses in the book, we have used logistic regression models to assess whether there is reliable evidence that particular variables are associated with each other.

Regression analysis aims to summarise the relationship between a 'dependent' variable and one or more 'independent' explanatory variables. It shows how well we can estimate a respondent's score on the dependent variable from knowledge of their scores on the independent variables. The technique takes into account relationships between the different independent variables (for example, between education and income, or social class and housing tenure). Regression is often undertaken to support a claim that the phenomena measured by the independent variables *cause* the phenomenon measured by the dependent variable. However, the causal ordering, if any, between the variables cannot be verified or falsified by the technique. Causality can only be inferred through special experimental designs or through assumptions made by the analyst.

Logistic regression is used to model variables which are dichotomous – for example, voting or not voting. An example can be found in Chapter 3 (Table 3.9) where the technique is used to investigate the characteristics of those who voted and those who did not vote in the elections to the Scottish Parliament. A number of characteristics which might explain turnout are included in the model (for example age, sex, social class, housing tenure, level of education and the party voted for in the 1997 general election). Although simple cross-tabulations may suggest that all of these characteristics are associated with turnout, because many are themselves associated with one another it is not possible to assess whether their association with turnout is 'real' or spurious. In this case the model identifies only two of the economic variables (education level and housing tenure) as having an independent significant effect on turnout as well as some of the other variables.

Full technical details of logistic regression can be found in many textbooks on social statistics, for example, Aitkin *et al.* (1989) and Bryman and Cramer (1997).

Factor analysis
Factor analysis is a statistical technique which aims to identify whether there are one or more apparent sources of commonality to the answers given by respondents to a set of questions. It ascertains the smallest number of factors (or dimensions) which can most economically summarise all of the variation found in the set of questions being analysed. Factors are established where respondents who give

a particular answer to one question in the set tend to give the same answer as each other to one or more of the other questions in the set. The technique is most useful when a relatively small number of factors is able to account for a relatively large proportion of the variance in all of the questions in the set.

The technique produces a factor loading for each question (or variable) on each factor. Where questions have a high loading on the same factor, it will be the case that respondents who give a particular answer to one of these questions tend to give a similar answer to the other questions. The technique is used in Chapter 7 to look at underlying dimensions to attitudes regarding the inclusion or exclusion of people with various characteristics in an independent Scotland.

NOTES

1. Group 1: Scottish Borders; Dumfries and Galloway; South Ayrshire; East Ayrshire, South Lanarkshire; North Ayrshire.
   Group 2: Inverclyde; West Dunbartonshire; Renfrewshire; East Renfrewshire; Glasgow City; East Dunbartonshire.
   Group 3: North Lanarkshire; Falkirk; West Lothian; Edinburgh; Midlothian; East Lothian.
   Group 4: Argyll and Bute; Stirling; Perth and Kinross; Clackmannanshire; Fife; Angus; Dundee.
   Group 5: Western Isles; Orkney; Shetland; Highland; Moray; Aberdeenshire; Aberdeen.

REFERENCES

Aitkin, M., Anderson, D., Francis, B. and Hinde, J. (1989), *Statistical Modelling in Glim*, Oxford: Oxford University Press.

Anderson, M. (2000), 'Control of immigration and exclusion', *Scottish Affairs*, no. 30, pp. 16–27.

Ashton, D. and Green, F. (1996), *Education, Training and the Global Economy*, Cheltenham: Edward Elgar.

Barnett, A. (1997), *This Time: Our Constitutional Revolution*, London: Vintage.

Billig, M. (1995), *Banal Nationalism*, London: Sage.

Bochel, H. and Denver, D. (1995), *Scottish Council Elections 1995: Results and Statistics*, Dundee: Election Studies.

Bochel, H. and Denver, D. (1999), *Scottish Council Elections 1999: Results and Statistics*, Dundee: Election Studies.

Bond, R. (2000), 'Squaring the circles; demonstrating and explaining the political "non-alignment" of Scottish national identity', *Scottish Affairs*, no. 32, pp. 15–35.

Brand, J., Mitchell, J. and Surridge, P. (1994), 'Social Constituency and Ideological Profile: Scottish nationalism in the 1990s', *Political Studies*, 42, pp. 616–29.

Brown, A. (1997), 'Scotland – paving the way for devolution?', *Parliamentary Affairs*, 50, pp. 658–71.

Brown, A. (1998), 'Deepening democracy: women and the Scottish parliament', *Regional and Federal Studies*, 8, pp. 103–19.

Brown, A. (1999), 'Taking their place in the new house: women and the Scottish Parliament', *Scottish Affairs*, no. 28, pp. 44–50.

183

Brown, A., McCrone, D. and Paterson, L. (1998), *Politics and Society in Scotland*, London: Macmillan, second edition.

Brown, A., McCrone, D., Paterson, L. and Surridge, P. (1999), *The Scottish Electorate: the 1997 General Election and Beyond*, London: Macmillan.

Bryman, A. and Cramer, D. (1997), *Quantitative Data Analysis*, London: Routledge.

Butler, D. and Westlake, M. (2000), *British Politics and European Elections 1999*, London: Macmillan.

Cavanagh, M., McGarvey, N. and Shephard, M. (2000), 'New Scottish Parliament, new Scottish Parliamentarians?', paper submitted for publication.

Consultative Steering Group (1998), *Shaping Scotland's Parliament*, Edinburgh: Scottish Office.

Curtice, J. (1988), 'One nation?', in R. Jowell, S. Witherspoon and L. Brook (eds), *British Social Attitudes: the Fifth Report*, Aldershot: Gower, pp. 127–54.

Curtice, J. (1996), 'One nation again?', in R. Jowell, J. Curtice, A. Park, L. Brook and K. Thomson (eds), *British Social Attitudes: the Thirteenth Report*, Aldershot: Gower, pp. 1–17.

Curtice, J. (2000), 'The new electoral politics', in G. Hassan and C. Warhurst (eds), *The New Scottish Politics*, Edinburgh: The Stationery Office, pp. 32–8.

Curtice, J. and Jowell, R. (1997), 'Is there really a demand for constitutional change?', in L. Paterson (ed.), *Understanding Constitutional Change*, special issue of *Scottish Affairs*, Edinburgh: Unit for the Study of Government in Scotland, pp. 61–92.

Curtice, J. and Steed, M. (1997), 'The results analysed', in D. Butler and D. Kavanaugh (eds), *The British General Election of 1997*, Basingstoke: Macmillan, pp. 295–325.

Curtice, J. and Steed, M. (2000), 'Appendix: an analysis of the result', in D. Butler and M. Westlake, *British Politics and European Elections*, London: Macmillan, pp. 240–56.

Denver, D. and MacAllister, I. (1999), 'The Scottish parliament elections 1999: an analysis of the results', *Scottish Affairs*, no. 28, pp. 10–31.

Denver D., Mitchell, J., Pattie, C. and Bochel, H. (2000), *Scotland Decides: The Devolution Issue and the Scottish Referendum*, London: Frank Cass.

Department for Education and Employment (1999), 'Blunkett welcomes Blair's higher education ambitions', press release, at www.dfee.gov.uk/news/99/428.htm.

DeVellis, R. F. (1991), *Scale Development: Theory and Applications*, Newbury Park, CA: Sage.

Dewar, D. (1998), 'The Scottish Parliament', in L. Paterson (ed.), *Understanding Constitutional Change*, special issue of *Scottish Affairs*, Edinburgh: Unit for the Study of Government in Scotland, pp. 4–12.

Dickson, M. (1994), 'Should auld acquaintance be forgot? A comparison of the Scots and English in Scotland', *Scottish Affairs*, no. 7, pp. 112–34.

Dunleavy, P., Margetts, H. and Weir, S. (1997), *Devolution Votes: PR Elections in Scotland and Wales*, Democratic Audit Paper No.12.

Dunleavy, P., Margetts, H., O'Duffy, B. and Weir, S. (1997), *Making Votes Count: Replaying the 1990s General Elections under Alternative Electoral Systems*, London: Charter 88.

Esping-Andersen, G. (1996), 'After the golden age? Welfare state dilemmas in a global economy', in G. Esping-Andersen (ed.), *Welfare States in Transition*, London: Sage, pp. 1–31.

Farrell, D. and Gallagher, M. (1999), 'British Voters and their Criteria for Evaluating Electoral Systems', *British Journal of Politics and International Relations*, 1, pp. 293–317.

Finnie, R. and McLeish, H. (1999), 'The negotiation diaries', *Scottish Affairs*, no. 28, pp. 51–61.

Gellner, E. (1983), *Nations and Nationalism*, Oxford: Blackwell.

Goldthorpe, J. (1996), 'Problems of "meritocracy"', in R. Erikson and J. O. Jonsson (eds), *Can Education be Equalised?*, Oxford: Westview, pp. 255–87.

Gore, S. and MacInnes, J. (2000), 'The politics of language in Catalonia', *Scottish Affairs*, no. 30, pp. 92–110.

Green, A. (1997), *Education, Globalisation and the Nation State*, London: Macmillan.

Gunther, R., Sani, G., and Shabad, G. (1986), *Spain After Franco: the Making of a Competitive Party System*, Berkeley: University of California Press.

Harvie, C. and Jones, P. (2000), *The Road to Home Rule*, Edinburgh: Polygon.

Hearn, J. (2000), *Claiming Scotland: National Identity and Liberal Culture*, Edinburgh: Polygon.

Heath, A. and Clifford, P. (1990), 'Class inequalities in education in the twentieth century', *Journal of the Royal Statistical Society*, series A, 153, pp. 1–16.

Heath, A., Evans, G. and Martin, J. (1994), 'The measurement of core beliefs and values', *British Journal of Political Science*, 24, pp. 115–31.

Heath, A., McLean, I., Taylor, B. and Curtice, J. (1999), 'Between first and second order: a comparison of voting behaviour in European and local elections in Britain', *European Journal of Political Research*, 35, pp. 389–414.

Heath, A., Taylor, B., Brook, L. and Park, A. (1999), 'British national sentiment', *British Journal of Political Science*, 29, pp. 155–75.

Hills, J. and Lelkes, O. (1999), 'Social security, selective universalism and patchwork redistribution', in R. Jowell, J. Curtice, A. Park and K. Thomson (eds), *British Social Attitudes: the Sixteenth Report*, Aldershot: Ashgate, pp. 1–22.

Himsworth, C. M. G. and Munro, C. R. (1998), *Devolution and the Scotland Bill*, Edinburgh: W. Green.

Hobsbawm, E. (1990), *Nations and Nationalism Since 1780: Programme, Myth and Reality*, Cambridge: Cambridge University Press.

Independent Committee of Inquiry into Student Finance (1999), *Student Finance: Fairness for the Future*, Edinburgh: The Stationery Office.

Jenkins Commission (1998), *Report of the Independent Commission on the Voting System*, chaired by Lord Jenkins, Cm 4090–I, London: The Stationery Office.

Jones, P. (1999), 'The 1999 Scottish parliament elections: from anti-Tory to anti-Nationalist politics', *Scottish Affairs*, no. 28, pp. 1–9.

Jowell, R., Curtice, J., Park, A., Brook, L., Thomson, K. and Bryson, C. (eds) (1998), *British – and European – Social Attitudes: the Fifteenth Report*, Aldershot: Ashgate.

Jowell, R., Curtice, J., Park, A. and Thomson, K. (eds) (1999a), *British Social Attitudes: the Sixteenth Report*, Aldershot: Ashgate.

Jowell, R., Curtice, J., Park, A. and Thomson, K. (1999b), 'Appendix 1', in R. Jowell, J. Curtice, A. Park and K. Thomson (eds), *British Social Attitudes: The Sixteenth Report*, Aldershot: Ashgate, pp. 235–53.

Keating, M. (1996), *Nations Against the State*, London: Macmillan.

Kellas, J., (1989), *The Scottish Political System* 4th edn, Cambridge: Cambridge University Press.

Leicester, G. (1996), 'Fundamentals for a new Scotland Act', *Scottish Affairs*, no. 16, pp. 1–6.

Marshall, G., Rose, D., Newby, H. and Vogler, C. (1988), *Social Class in Modern Britain*, London: Unwin Hyman.

McCrone, D. (1992), *Understanding Scotland: the Sociology of a Stateless Nation*, London: Routledge.

McCrone, D. (1998), *The Sociology of Nationalism*, London: Routledge.

McCrone, D. (1999), 'Opinion polls in Scotland, July 1998–June 1999', *Scottish Affairs*, no. 28, pp. 32–43.

Miller, W. (1988), *Irrelevant Elections? The Quality of Local Democracy in Britain*, Oxford: Oxford University Press.

Moreno, L. (1988) 'Scotland and Catalonia: the path to home rule', in D. McCrone and A. Brown (eds), *The Scottish Government Yearbook*, Edinburgh: Unit for the Study of Government in Scotland, pp. 166–81.

Moreno, L. and Arriba, A. (1996), 'Dual identity in autonomous Catalonia', *Scottish Affairs*, no. 17, pp. 78–97.

Morton, G. (1999), *Unionist Nationalism: Governing Urban Scotland, 1830–1860*, East Linton: Tuckwell Press.

Paterson, L. (1991), 'Ane end of ane auld sang: sovereignty and the renegotiation of the Union' in D. McCrone and A. Brown (eds), *The Scottish*

Government Yearbook 1991, Edinburgh: Unit for the Study of Government in Scotland, pp. 104–22.

Paterson, L. (1994), *The Autonomy of Modern Scotland*, Edinburgh: Edinburgh University Press.

Paterson, L. (1997), 'Policy making in Scottish education: a case of pragmatic nationalism', in P. Munn and M. Clark (eds), *Education in Scotland*, London: Routledge, pp. 138–55.

Paterson, L. (1998), *A Diverse Assembly: the Debate on a Scottish Parliament*, Edinburgh: Edinburgh University Press.

Paterson, L. (2000a), 'Scottish democracy and Scottish utopias: the first year of the Scottish parliament', *Scottish Affairs*, no. 33, pp. 45–61.

Paterson, L. (2000b), *Education and the Scottish Parliament*, Edinburgh: Dunedin Academic Press.

Paterson, L. (2000c), 'The social class of Catholics in Scotland', *Statistics in Society, Journal of the Royal Statistical Society* (Series A), 163, pp. 363–79.

Paterson, L. (2000d), *Crisis in the Classroom: the Exam Debacle and the Way Ahead for Scottish Education*, Edinburgh: Mainstream.

Pierson, C. (1991), *Beyond the Welfare State?*, Cambridge: Polity.

Raffe, D. (1985), 'The extendable ladder: Scotland's 16+ Action Plan', *Youth and Policy*, no.12, pp. 27–33.

Rallings, C. and Thrasher, M. (1997), *Local Elections in Britain*, London: Routledge.

Reif, K. (1984), 'National electoral cycles and European elections 1979 and 1984', *Electoral Studies*, 3, pp. 244–55.

Reif, K. and Schmitt, H. (1980), 'Nine national second-order elections', in K. Reif (ed.), *Ten European Elections: Campaigns and Results of the 1979/81 First Direct Elections to the European Parliament*, Aldershot: Gower, pp. 3–44.

Rosie, M. and McCrone, D. (2000), 'The past is history: Catholics in modern Scotland', in T. Devine (ed.), *Scotland's Shames? Bigotry, Sectarianism and Catholicism in Modern Scotland*, Edinburgh: Mainstream, pp. 199–218.

Schleicher, K. (ed.) (1993), *Nationalism in Education*, Frankfurt: Peter Lang.

Scotland Office (2000), *Assessment of the Voter Education Campaign for the Scottish Parliamentary Elections*, Edinburgh: The Stationery Office.

Scottish Constitutional Convention (1995), *Scotland's Parliament, Scotland's Right*, Edinburgh: Cosla.

Scottish Executive (1999), *Students in Higher Education in Scotland*, statistical bulletin, at www.scotland.gov.uk/stats/educ.htm

Scottish Executive (2000), *Scotland the Learning Nation: Helping Students*, Consultation Paper, May, Edinburgh: Scottish Executive.

Scottish Office (1995), *Views on Scottish Education and International Comparisons*, Edinburgh: HMSO.

Scottish Office (1997), *Scotland's Parliament*, Cm 3658, Edinburgh: Stationery Office.

Scottish Office (1999), *Factsheet 1: The Scottish Parliament*.

Spector, P. E. (1992), *Summated Rating Scale Construction: an Introduction*, Newbury Park, CA: Sage.

Stationery Office (1998), *The Scotland Act 1998*, London: The Stationery Office.

Steel, D. (1999), 'Foreword', *Scottish Parliament: Opening Ceremony*.

Swaddle, K. and Heath, A. (1989), 'Official and reported turnout in the British general election of 1987', *British Journal of Political Science*, 19, pp. 537–70.

Taylor, B. (1999), *The Scottish Parliament*, Edinburgh: Polygon at Edinburgh.

Thomson, K., Park, A. and Brook, L. (1999), *British General Election Study, 1997: Cross-section survey, Scottish Election Study and Ethnic Minority Election Study: Technical Report*, London: National Centre for Social Research.

Thomson, K., Park, A. and Bryson, C. (2000), *The Scottish and Welsh Referendum Studies 1997: Technical Report*, London: National Centre for Social Research.

Van der Eijk, C., and Franklin, M. (1996), *Choosing Europe? The European Electorate and National Politics in the Face of Union*, Ann Arbor: University of Michigan Press.

Verba, S. and Nie, N. H. (1972), *Participation in America*, New York: Harper and Row.

Weir, A. D. (1988), *Education and Vocation: 14–18*, Edinburgh: Scottish Academic Press.

Wright, Kenyon (1997), *The People Say Yes*, Argyll: Argyll Publishing.

INDEX

189

national identity and, 109–12
party identification, 176
support for devolution by, 85–6,
115
welfare views, 130–2
power sharing, 93
primary education, 150–1, 154–5
private schools, 150–1
proportional representation (PR)
Additional Member System of,
11, 14, 21, 67, 81
coalition governments, 72, 73–4
criticism of, 73–6
first national elections in Britain,
2, 66
voter understanding and
acceptance of, 68–77, 165
Westminster Parliament and, 76–7
Protestants, 56, 62, 86–7, 158
public spending, 125
public welfare, 124–30, 133–4

Quebec, 6, 146

redistribution of wealth, 124, 126–7,
128, 131–2, 134–5, 142, 163
referendum 1997, 5, 8–9, 102, 145,
172–3
campaign, 13–14
regional ballot, 14, 18–19, 21, 31, 32,
67
and constituency vote, 78–82
and Labour vote, 139
religion
education and, 146, 150–1,
157–8
SNP vs. Labour voting, 62, 63,
64
support for devolution, 86–7
voter turnout, 50–2, 55–6
representation, 74–5
retirement, 125, 129
Robertson, George, 10
Roman Catholics, 56, 62, 63, 146

education, 150–1, 157–8
and support for devolution, 86–7

Salmond, Alex, 17–18, 25, 38,
39–40, 42
Scotland
constitutional question and,
38–40, 164–5
educational policy in, 147–52
Labour vote in, 136–40
views of redistribution, 126–7
views on public spending, 125
views on social welfare, 124–9
Scotland Act (1998), 9, 14, 23
Scotland Forward campaign, 13, 145
Scottish citizenship, criteria for,
118–19
Scottish Constitutional Convention
(SCC), 10–12
Scottish Election Surveys, 172–3
Scottish identity, 165–6
criteria for, 117–19
education and, 145, 146, 147,
152–7
and English conflict, 116–17
measurements of, 104–8
Scottish National Party and,
115–16
Scottish National Party (SNP) and
voters
absence from the Convention, 12
Additional Member System, 67
during election campaign, 17–18
election results, 19–20, 21–2,
32–3
flow of the vote, 48–9
future of, 162–3
gender balance in candidate
selection, 16
Labour Party and, 59–64
left-wing politics, 122, 123
national identity and, 109–12,
115–16
party proportionality, 2, 66

Related Reading from Polygon at Edinburgh

Year Zero

An Inside View of the Scottish Parliament
Mike Watson, MSP
1 902930 26 6   224pp   £12.99

Everybody has an opinion about the new Scottish Parliament. What it has achieved, what it ought to be achieving and the mistakes made in its first year have been debated in the media on a regular basis. But this is only one side of the story, a view from the outside. This book offers the reader an insight to the inner workings of the Parliament, and a hands-on, insider view of the events witnessed during its first year.

Mike Watson asks whether the Parliament has delivered what it promised the people of Scotland - a modern, accessible, transparent and responsive legislature, quite unlike Westminster - and he explores the extent to which the new Parliament's aims and powers were realistically set, illustrating the ways in which it has reacted to the unpredictability of events.

The Scottish Parliament

Brian Taylor
1 902930 12 6   226pp   £12.99

This important book provides an invaluable guide to Scotland's new Parliament.

With his unique insight, gained in more than twenty years of covering Scottish politics as a journalist, Brian Taylor offers an analysis of the background and motivations for the most monumental political change in Scotland since the Union. Taylor examines the popular motivation for devolution - and traces in detail the practical steps which led to the establishment of Scotland's new Parliament. In addition, he provides a challenging assessment of Scotland's political future: tackling the issue of whether devolution will content the Scots.

Order from
Polygon at Edinburgh,
22 George Square, Edinburgh, EH8 9LF
Email: polygon.press@eup.ed.ac.uk

Visit our website www.eup.ed.ac.uk

All details correct at time of printing but subject to change without notice